THE CONSOLATION OF PHILOSOPHY OF BOETHIUS

THE CONSOLATION OF PHILOSOPHY OF BOETHIUS

ANICIUS MANLIUS SEVERINUS BOETHIUS
TRANSLATED BY
H. R. JAMES, M.A., CH. CH. OXFORD

GYAN

Published by

Gyan Publishing House
5, Ansari Road
Daryaganj, New Delhi-110002
Phone: 011-47034999, 9811692060
E-mail: books@gyanbooks.com

Distribution Network
gyanbooks.com
India, USA, Canada, UK, Australia, France

ISBN: 978-81-212-8612-1 (PB)
First Published, 1897

2nd Impression 2023

Printed at: Gyan Press, Delhi.

THE CONSOLATION OF PHILOSOPHY OF BOETHIUS
Author: Anicius Manlius Severinus Boethius, Translator: H. R. James

ὅμως δὲ καὶ ἐν τούτοις διαλάμπει τὸ καλὸν, ἐπειδὰν φέρῃ τις εὐκόλως πολλὰς καὶ μεγάλας ἀτυχίας, μὴ δι' ἀναλγησίαν, ἀλλὰ γεννάδας ὢν καὶ μεγαλόψυχος.

Aristotle's 'Ethics,' I., xi. 12.

Diptych representing Narius Manlius Boethius, father of Anicius Manlius Severinus Boethius. The inscription in full would run thus :—

NARivs MANLivs BOETHIVS Vir Clarissimvs ET INLvstris
EXPraefectvs Praetorio Praefectvs VrbiS· Et
Comes Consvl ORDinarivs ET PATRICivs

(*For description vid. Preface, p. vi.*)

THE

CONSOLATION OF PHILOSOPHY OF BOETHIUS.

Translated into English Prose and Verse

BY

H. R. JAMES, M.A.,
CH. CH. OXFORD.

Quantumlibet igitur sæviant mali, sapienti tamen corona non decidet, non arescet.

Melioribus animum conformaveris, nihil opus est judice præmium deferente, tu te ipse excellentioribus addidisti; studium ad pejora deflexeris, extra ne quæsieris ultorem, tu te ipse in deteriora trusisti.

LONDON:
ELLIOT STOCK, 62, PATERNOSTER ROW.
1897.

PREFACE.

THE book called 'The Consolation of Philosophy' was throughout the Middle Ages, and down to the beginnings of the modern epoch in the sixteenth century, the scholar's familiar companion. Few books have exercised a wider influence in their time. It has been translated into every European tongue, and into English nearly a dozen times, from King Alfred's paraphrase to the translations of Lord Preston, Causton, Ridpath, and Duncan, in the eighteenth century. The belief that what once pleased so widely must still have some charm is my excuse for attempting the present translation. The great work of Boethius, with its alternate prose and verse, skilfully fitted together like dialogue and chorus in a Greek play, is unique in literature, and has a pathetic interest from the time and circumstances of its composition. It ought not to be forgotten. Those who can go to the original will find their reward. There may be room also for a new translation in English after an interval of close on a hundred years.

Some of the editions contain a reproduction of a bust purporting to represent Boethius. Lord Preston's translation, for example, has such a portrait, which it refers to an original in marble at Rome. This I have been unable to trace, and suspect that it is apocryphal. The Hope Collection at Oxford contains a completely different portrait in a print, which gives no authority. I have ventured to use as a frontispiece a reproduction from a plaster-cast in the Ashmolean Museum, taken from an ivory diptych preserved in the Bibliotheca Quiriniana at Brescia, which represents Narius Manlius Boethius, the father of the philosopher. Portraiture of this period is so rare that it seemed that, failing a likeness of the author himself, this authentic representation of his father might have interest, as giving the consular dress and insignia of the time, and also as illustrating the decadence of contemporary art. The consul wears a richly-embroidered cloak; his right hand holds a staff surmounted by the Roman eagle, his left the *mappa circensis*, or napkin used for starting the races in the circus; at his feet are palms and bags of money—prizes for the victors in the games. For permission to use this cast my thanks are due to the authorities of the Ashmolean Museum, as also to Mr. T. W. Jackson, Curator of the Hope Collection, who first called my attention to its existence.

I have to thank my brother, Mr. L. James, of Radley College, for much valuable help and for correcting the proof-sheets of the translation. The text used is that of Peiper, Leipsic, 1874.

PROEM.

ANICIUS MANLIUS SEVERINUS BOETHIUS lived in the last quarter of the fifth century A.D., and the first quarter of the sixth. He was growing to manhood, when Theodoric, the famous Ostrogoth, crossed the Alps and made himself master of Italy. Boethius belonged to an ancient family, which boasted a connection with the legendary glories of the Republic, and was still among the foremost in wealth and dignity in the days of Rome's abasement. His parents dying early, he was brought up by Symmachus, whom the age agreed to regard as of almost saintly character, and afterwards became his son-in-law. His varied gifts, aided by an excellent education, won for him the reputation of the most accomplished man of his time. He was orator, poet, musician, philosopher. It is his peculiar distinction to have handed on to the Middle Ages the tradition of Greek philosophy by his Latin translations of the works of Aristotle. Called early to a public career, the highest honours of the State came to him unsought. He was sole Consul in 510 A.D., and was ultimately raised by Theodoric to the dignity of Magister Officiorum, or head of the whole civil administration. He was no less happy in his domestic life, in the virtues of his wife, Rusticiana, and the fair promise of his two sons, Symmachus and Boethius; happy also in the society of a refined circle of friends. Noble, wealthy, accomplished, universally esteemed for his virtues, high in the favour of the Gothic King, he appeared to all men a signal example of the union of merit and good fortune. His felicity seemed to culminate in the year 522 A.D., when, by special and extraordinary favour, his two sons, young as they were for so exalted an honour, were created joint Consuls and rode to the senate-house attended by a throng of senators, and the acclamations of the multitude. Boethius himself, amid the general applause, delivered the public speech in the King's honour usual on such occasions. Within a year he was a solitary prisoner at Pavia, stripped of honours, wealth, and friends, with death hanging over him, and a terror worse than death, in the fear lest those dearest to him should be involved in the worst results of his downfall. It is in this situation that the opening of the 'Consolation of Philosophy' brings Boethius before us. He represents himself as seated in his prison distraught with grief, indignant at the injustice of his misfortunes, and seeking relief for his melancholy in writing verses descriptive of his condition. Suddenly there appears to him the Divine figure of Philosophy, in the guise of a woman of superhuman dignity and beauty, who by a succession of discourses convinces him of the vanity of regret for the lost gifts of fortune, raises his mind once more to the contemplation of the true good, and makes clear to him the mystery of the world's moral government.

INDEX

OF

VERSE INTERLUDES.

BOOK I.

THE SORROWS OF BOETHIUS.

BOOK II.

THE VANITY OF FORTUNE'S GIFTS.

BOOK III.

TRUE HAPPINESS AND FALSE.

BOOK IV.

GOOD AND ILL FORTUNE.

BOOK V.

FREE WILL AND GOD'S FORE-KNOWLEDGE.

REFERENCES TO QUOTATIONS IN THE TEXT.

Bk. I., ch. iv., p. 17, l. 6: 'Iliad,' I. 363.
,, ch. iv., p. 18, l. 7: Plato, 'Republic,' V. 473, D; Jowett, vol. iii., pp. 170, 171 (3rd edit.).
,, ch. iv., p. 22, l. 6: Plato, 'Republic,' I. 347, C; Jowett, III., p. 25.
,, ch. v., p. 30, l. 19: 'Iliad,' II., 204, 205.
Bk. II., ch. ii., p. 50, l. 21: 'Iliad,' XXIV. 527, 528.
,, ch. vii., p. 78, l. 25: Cicero, 'De Republicâ,' VI. 20, in the 'Somnium Scipionis.'
Bk. III., ch. iv., p. 106, l. 10: Catullus, LII., 2.
,, ch. vi., p. 114, l. 4: Euripides, 'Andromache,' 319, 320.
,, ch. ix., p. 129, l. 3: Plato, 'Timæus,' 27, C; Jowett, vol. iii., p. 448.
,, ch. xii., p. 157, l. 14: Quoted Plato, 'Sophistes,' 244, E; Jowett, vol. iv., p. 374.
,, ch. xii., p. 157, l. 22: Plato, 'Timæus,' 29, B; Jowett, vol. iii., p. 449.
Bk. IV., ch. vi., p. 206, l. 17: Lucan, 'Pharsalia,' I. 126.
,, ch. vi., p. 210, l. 23: 'Iliad,' XII. 176.
Bk. V., ch. i., p. 227, l. 16: Aristotle, 'Physics,' II. v. 5.
,, ch. iii., p. 238, l. 20: Horace, 'Satires,' II. v. 59.
,, ch. iv., p. 243, l. 3: Cicero, 'De Divinatione,' II. 7, 8.
,, ch. vi., p. 258, l. 8: Aristotle, 'De Cælo,' II. 1.

BOOK I.

THE SORROWS OF BOETHIUS.

SUMMARY.

Boethius' complaint (Song I.).—Ch. I. Philosophy appears to Boethius, drives away the Muses of Poetry, and herself laments (Song II.) the disordered condition of his mind.—Ch. II. Boethius is speechless with amazement. Philosophy wipes away the tears that have clouded his eyesight.—Ch. III. Boethius recognises his mistress Philosophy. To his wondering inquiries she explains her presence, and recalls to his mind the persecutions to which Philosophy has oftentimes from of old been subjected by an ignorant world.—Ch. IV. Philosophy bids Boethius declare his griefs. He relates the story of his unjust accusation and ruin. He concludes with a prayer (Song V.) that the moral disorder in human affairs may be set right.—Ch. V. Philosophy admits the justice of Boethius' self-vindication, but grieves rather for the unhappy change in his mind. She will first tranquillize his spirit by soothing remedies. —CH. VI. Philosophy tests Boethius' mental state by certain questions, and discovers three chief causes of his soul's sickness: (1) He has forgotten his own true nature; (2) he knows not the end towards which the whole universe tends; (3) he knows not the means by which the world is governed.

BOOK I.

SONG I.

Boethius' Complaint.

I WHO wrought my studious numbers
Smoothly once in happier days,
Now perforce in tears and sadness
Learn a mournful strain to raise.
Lo, the Muses, grief-dishevelled,
Guide my pen and voice my woe;
Down their cheeks unfeigned the tear drops
To my sad complainings flow!
These alone in danger's hour
Faithful found, have dared attend
On the footsteps of the exile
To his lonely journey's end.

These that were the pride and pleasure
  Of my youth and high estate
Still remain the only solace
  Of the old man's mournful fate.
Old? Ah yes; swift, ere I knew it,
  By these sorrows on me pressed
Age hath come; lo, Grief hath bid me
  Wear the garb that fits her best.
O'er my head untimely sprinkled
  These white hairs my woes proclaim,
And the skin hangs loose and shrivelled
  On this sorrow-shrunken frame.
Blest is death that intervenes not
  In the sweet, sweet years of peace,
But unto the broken-hearted,
  When they call him, brings release!
Yet Death passes by the wretched,
  Shuts his ear and slumbers deep;
Will not heed the cry of anguish,
  Will not close the eyes that weep.
For, while yet inconstant Fortune
  Poured her gifts and all was bright,
Death's dark hour had all but whelmed
    me
  In the gloom of endless night.
Now, because misfortune's shadow
  Hath o'erclouded that false face,

Cruel Life still halts and lingers,
  Though I loathe his weary race.
Friends, why did ye once so lightly
  Vaunt me happy among men?
Surely he who so hath fallen
  Was not firmly founded then.

I.

While I was thus mutely pondering within myself, and recording my sorrowful complainings with my pen, it seemed to me that there appeared above my head a woman of a countenance exceeding venerable. Her eyes were bright as fire, and of a more than human keenness; her complexion was lively, her vigour showed no trace of enfeeblement; and yet her years were right full, and she plainly seemed not of our age and time. Her stature was difficult to judge. At one moment it exceeded not the common height, at another her forehead seemed to strike the sky; and whenever she raised her head higher, she began to pierce within the very heavens, and to baffle the eyes of them that looked upon her. Her garments were of an imperishable fabric, wrought with the finest threads and of the most delicate workmanship; and these, as her own lips afterwards assured me, she had herself woven with her own hands. The beauty of this vesture had been somewhat tarnished by age and neglect, and wore that dingy look which marble contracts from exposure. On the lowermost edge was inwoven the Greek letter Π, on the topmost the letter Θ,* and between the two were to be seen steps, like a staircase, from the lower to the upper letter. This robe, moreover, had been torn by the hands of violent persons, who had each snatched away what he could clutch.† Her right hand held a note-book; in her left she bore a staff. And when she saw the Muses of Poesie standing by my bedside, dictating the words of my lamentations, she was moved awhile to wrath, and her eyes flashed sternly. 'Who,' said she, 'has allowed yon play-acting wantons to approach this sick man—these who, so far

* Π (P) stands for the Political life, the life of action; Θ (Th) for the Theoretical life, the life of thought.

† The Stoic, Epicurean, and other philosophical sects, which Boethius regards as heterodox. See also below, ch. iii., p. 14.

from giving medicine to heal his malady, even feed it with sweet poison? These it is who kill the rich crop of reason with the barren thorns of passion, who accustom men's minds to disease, instead of setting them free. Now, were it some common man whom your allurements were seducing, as is usually your way, I should be less indignant. On such a one I should not have spent my pains for naught. But this is one nurtured in the Eleatic and Academic philosophies. Nay, get ye gone, ye sirens, whose sweetness lasteth not; leave him for my muses to tend and heal!' At these words of upbraiding, the whole band, in deepened sadness, with downcast eyes, and blushes that confessed their shame, dolefully left the chamber.

But I, because my sight was dimmed with much weeping, and I could not tell who was this woman of authority so commanding—I was dumfoundered, and, with my gaze fastened on the earth, continued silently to await what she might do next. Then she drew near me and sat on the edge of my couch, and, looking into my face all heavy with grief and fixed in sadness on the ground, she bewailed in these words the disorder of my mind:

SONG II.

His Despondency.

Alas! in what abyss his mind
  Is plunged, how wildly tossed!
Still, still towards the outer night
  She sinks, her true light lost,
As oft as, lashed tumultuously
By earth-born blasts, care's waves rise high.

Yet once he ranged the open heavens,
  The sun's bright pathway tracked;
Watched how the cold moon waxed and
    waned;
  Nor rested, till there lacked
To his wide ken no star that steers
Amid the maze of circling spheres.

The causes why the blusterous winds
  Vex ocean's tranquil face,
Whose hand doth turn the stable globe,
  Or why his even race
From out the ruddy east the sun
Unto the western waves doth run:

What is it tempers cunningly
  The placid hours of spring,
So that it blossoms with the rose
  For earth's engarlanding:
Who loads the year's maturer prime
With clustered grapes in autumn time:

All this he knew—thus ever strove
  Deep Nature's lore to guess.
Now, reft of reason's light, he lies,
  And bonds his neck oppress;
While by the heavy load constrained,
His eyes to this dull earth are chained.

II.

'But the time,' said she, 'calls rather for healing than for lamentation.' Then, with her eyes bent full upon me, 'Art thou that man,' she cries, 'who, erstwhile fed with the milk and reared upon the nourishment which is mine to give, had grown up to the full vigour of a manly spirit? And yet I had bestowed such armour on thee as would have proved an invincible defence, hadst thou not first cast it away. Dost thou know me? Why art thou silent? Is it shame or amazement that hath struck thee dumb? Would it were shame; but, as I see, a stupor hath seized upon thee.' Then, when she saw me not only answering nothing, but mute and utterly incapable of speech, she gently touched my breast with her hand, and said: 'There is no danger; these are the symptoms of lethargy, the usual sickness of deluded minds. For awhile he has forgotten himself; he will easily recover his memory, if only he first recognises me. And that he may do so, let me now wipe his eyes that are clouded with a mist of mortal things.' Thereat, with a fold of her robe, she dried my eyes all swimming with tears.

SONG III.

The Mists dispelled.

Then the gloom of night was scattered,
  Sight returned unto mine eyes.
So, when haply rainy Caurus
  Rolls the storm-clouds through the skies,
Hidden is the sun; all heaven
  Is obscured in starless night.
But if, in wild onset sweeping,
  Boreas frees day's prisoned light,
All suddenly the radiant god outstreams,
And strikes our dazzled eyesight with his beams.

III.

Even so the clouds of my melancholy were broken up. I saw the clear sky, and regained the power to recognise the face of my physician. Accordingly, when I had lifted my eyes and fixed my gaze upon her, I beheld my nurse, Philosophy, whose halls I had frequented from my youth up.

'Ah! why,' I cried, 'mistress of all excellence, hast thou come down from on high, and entered the solitude of this my exile? Is it that thou, too, even as I, mayst be persecuted with false accusations?'

'Could I desert thee, child,' said she, 'and not lighten the burden which thou hast taken upon thee through the hatred of my name, by sharing this trouble? Even forgetting that it were not lawful for Philosophy to leave companionless the way of the innocent, should I, thinkest thou, fear to incur reproach, or shrink from it, as though some strange new thing had befallen? Thinkest thou that now, for the first time in an evil age, Wisdom hath been assailed by peril? Did I not often in days of old, before my servant Plato lived, wage stern warfare with the rashness of folly? In his lifetime, too, Socrates, his master, won with my aid the victory of an unjust death. And when, one after the other, the Epicurean herd, the Stoic, and the rest, each of them as far as in them lay, went about to seize the heritage he left, and were dragging me off protesting and resisting, as their booty, they tore in pieces the garment which I had woven with my own hands, and, clutching the torn pieces, went off, believing that the whole of me had passed into their possession. And some of them, because some traces of my vesture were seen upon them, were destroyed through the mistake of the lewd multitude, who falsely deemed them to be my disciples. It may be thou knowest not of the banishment of Anaxagoras, of the poison draught of Socrates, nor of Zeno's torturing, because these things happened in a distant country; yet mightest thou have learnt the fate of Arrius, of Seneca, of Soranus, whose stories are neither old nor unknown to fame. These men were brought to destruction for no other reason than that, settled as they were in my principles, their lives were a manifest contrast to the ways of the wicked. So there is nothing thou shouldst wonder at, if on the seas of this life we are tossed by storm-blasts, seeing that we have made it our chiefest aim to refuse compliance with evil-doers. And though, maybe, the host of the wicked is many in number, yet is it contemptible, since it is under no leadership, but is hurried hither and thither at the blind driving of mad error. And if at times and seasons they set in array against us, and fall on in overwhelming strength, our leader draws off her forces into the citadel while they are busy plundering the useless baggage. But we from our vantage ground, safe from all this wild work, laugh to see them making prize of the most valueless of things, protected by a bulwark which aggressive folly may not aspire to reach.'

SONG IV.

Nothing can subdue Virtue.

Whoso calm, serene, sedate,
Sets his foot on haughty fate ;
Firm and steadfast, come what will,
Keeps his mien unconquered still ;
Him the rage of furious seas,
Tossing high wild menaces,
Nor the flames from smoky forges
That Vesuvius disgorges,
Nor the bolt that from the sky
Smites the tower, can terrify.
Why, then, shouldst thou feel affright
At the tyrant's weakling might ?
Dread him not, nor fear no harm,
And thou shalt his rage disarm ;
But who to hope or fear gives way—
Lost his bosom's rightful sway—
He hath cast away his shield,
Like a coward fled the field ;
He hath forged all unaware
Fetters his own neck must bear !

IV.

'Dost thou understand?' she asks. Do my words sink into thy mind? Or art thou dull "as the ass to the sound of the lyre"? Why dost thou weep? Why do tears stream from thy eyes?

'"Speak out, hide it not in thy heart."

If thou lookest for the physician's help, thou must needs disclose thy wound.'

Then I, gathering together what strength I could, began: 'Is there still need of telling? Is not the cruelty of fortune against me plain enough? Doth not the very aspect of this place move thee? Is this the library, the room which thou hadst chosen as thy constant resort in my home, the place where we so often sat together and held discourse of all things in heaven and earth? Was my garb and mien like this when I explored with thee nature's hid secrets, and thou didst trace for me with thy wand the courses of the stars, moulding the while my character and the whole conduct of my life after the pattern of the celestial order? Is this the recompense of my obedience? Yet thou hast enjoined by Plato's mouth the maxim, "that states would be happy, either if philosophers ruled them, or if it should so befall that their rulers would turn philosophers." By his mouth likewise thou didst point out this imperative reason why philosophers should enter public life, to wit, lest, if the reins of government be left to unprincipled and profligate citizens, trouble and destruction should come upon the good. Following these precepts, I have tried to apply in the business of public administration the principles which I learnt from thee in leisured seclusion. Thou art my witness and that divinity who hath implanted thee in the hearts of the wise, that I brought to my duties no aim but zeal for the public good. For this cause I have become involved in bitter and irreconcilable feuds, and, as happens inevitably, if a man holds fast to the independence of conscience, I have had to think nothing of giving offence to the powerful in the cause of justice. How often have I encountered and balked Conigastus in his assaults on the fortunes of the weak? How often have I thwarted Trigguilla, steward of the king's household, even when his villainous schemes were as good as accomplished? How often have I risked my position and influence to protect poor wretches from the false charges innumerable with which they were for ever being harassed by the greed and license of the barbarians? No one has ever drawn me aside from justice to oppression. When ruin was overtaking the fortunes of the provincials through the combined pressure of private rapine and public taxation, I grieved no less than the sufferers. When at a season of grievous scarcity a forced sale, disastrous as it was unjustifiable, was proclaimed, and threatened to overwhelm Campania with starvation, I embarked on a struggle with the prætorian prefect in the public interest, I fought the case at the king's judgment-seat, and succeeded in preventing the enforcement of the sale. I rescued the consular Paulinus from the gaping jaws of the court bloodhounds, who in their covetous hopes had already made short work of his wealth. To save Albinus, who was of the same exalted rank, from the penalties of a prejudged charge, I exposed myself to the hatred of Cyprian, the informer.

'Thinkest thou I had laid up for myself store of enmities enough? Well, with the rest of my countrymen, at any rate, my safety should have been assured, since my love of justice had left me no hope of security at court. Yet who was it brought the charges by which I have been struck down? Why, one of my accusers is Basil, who, after being dismissed from the king's household, was driven by his debts to lodge an information against my name. There is Opilio, there is Gaudentius, men who for many and various offences the king's sentence had condemned to banishment; and when they declined to obey, and sought to save themselves by taking sanctuary, the king, as soon as he heard of it, decreed that, if they did not depart from the city of Ravenna within a prescribed time, they should be branded on the forehead and expelled. What would exceed the rigour of this severity? And yet on that same day these very men lodged an information against me, and the information was admitted. Just Heaven! had I deserved this by my way of life? Did it make them fit accusers that my condemnation was a foregone conclusion? Has fortune no shame—if not at the accusation of the innocent, at least for the vileness of the accusers? Perhaps thou wonderest what is the sum of the charges laid against me? I wished, they say, to save the senate. But how? I am accused of hindering an informer from producing evidence to prove the senate guilty of treason. Tell me, then, what is thy counsel, O my mistress. Shall I deny the charge, lest I bring shame on thee? But I did wish it, and I shall never cease to wish it. Shall I admit it? Then the work of thwarting the informer will come to an end. Shall I call the wish for the preservation of that illustrious house a crime? Of a truth the senate, by its decrees concerning me, has made it such! But blind folly, though it deceive itself with false names, cannot alter the true merits of things, and, mindful of the precept of Socrates, I do not think it right either to keep the truth concealed or allow falsehood to pass. But this, however it may be, I leave to thy judgment and to the verdict of the discerning. Moreover, lest the course of events and the true facts should be hidden from posterity, I have myself committed to writing an account of the transaction.

'What need to speak of the forged letters by which an attempt is made to prove that I hoped for the freedom of Rome? Their falsity would have been manifest, if I had been allowed to use the confession of the informers themselves, evidence which has in all matters the most convincing force. Why, what hope of freedom is left to us? Would there were any! I should have answered with the epigram of Canius when Caligula declared him to have been cognisant of a conspiracy against him. "If I had known," said he, "thou shouldst never have known." Grief hath not so blunted my perceptions in this matter that I should complain because impious wretches contrive their villainies against the virtuous, but at their achievement of their hopes I do exceedingly marvel. For evil purposes are, perchance, due to the imperfection of human nature; that it should be possible for scoundrels to carry out their worst schemes against the innocent, while God beholdeth, is verily monstrous. For this cause, not without reason, one of thy disciples asked, "If God exists, whence comes evil? Yet whence comes good, if He exists not?" However, it might well be that wretches who seek the blood of all honest men and of the whole senate should wish to destroy me also, whom they saw to be a bulwark of the senate and all honest men. But did I deserve such a fate from the Fathers also? Thou rememberest, methinks—since thou didst ever stand by my side to direct what I should do or say—thou rememberest, I say, how at Verona, when the king, eager for the general destruction, was bent on implicating the whole senatorial order in the charge of treason brought against Albinus, with what indifference to my own peril I maintained the innocence of its members, one and all. Thou knowest that what I say is the truth, and that I have never boasted of my good deeds in a spirit of self-praise. For whenever a man by proclaiming his good deeds receives the recompense of fame, he diminishes in a measure the secret reward of a good conscience. What issues have overtaken my innocency thou seest. Instead of reaping the rewards of true virtue, I undergo the penalties of a guilt falsely laid to my charge—nay, more than this; never did an open confession of guilt cause such unanimous severity among the assessors, but that some consideration, either of the mere frailty of human nature, or of fortune's universal instability, availed to soften the verdict of some few. Had I been accused of a design to fire the temples, to slaughter the priests with impious sword, of plotting the massacre of all honest men, I should yet have been produced in court, and only punished on due confession or conviction. Now for my too great zeal towards the senate I have been condemned to outlawry and death, unheard and undefended, at a distance of near five hundred miles away.* Oh, my judges, well do ye deserve that no one should hereafter be convicted of a fault like mine!

'Yet even my very accusers saw how honourable was the charge they brought against me, and, in order to overlay it with some shadow of guilt, they falsely asserted that in the pursuit of my ambition I had stained my conscience with sacrilegious acts. And yet thy spirit, indwelling in me, had driven from the chamber of my soul all lust of earthly success, and with thine eye ever upon me, there could be no place left for sacrilege. For thou didst daily repeat in my ear and instil into my mind the Pythagorean maxim, "Follow after God." It was not likely, then, that I should covet the assistance of the vilest spirits, when thou wert

* The distance from Rome to Pavia, the place of Boethius' imprisonment, is 455 Roman miles.

moulding me to such an excellence as should conform me to the likeness of God. Again, the innocency of the inner sanctuary of my home, the company of friends of the highest probity, a father-in-law revered at once for his pure character and his active beneficence, shield me from the very suspicion of sacrilege. Yet—atrocious as it is—they even draw credence for this charge from *thee*; I am like to be thought implicated in wickedness on this very account, that I am imbued with *thy* teachings and stablished in *thy* ways. So it is not enough that my devotion to thee should profit me nothing, but thou also must be assailed by reason of the odium which I have incurred. Verily this is the very crown of my misfortunes, that men's opinions for the most part look not to real merit, but to the event; and only recognise foresight where Fortune has crowned the issue with her approval. Whereby it comes to pass that reputation is the first of all things to abandon the unfortunate. I remember with chagrin how perverse is popular report, how various and discordant men's judgments. This only will I say, that the most crushing of misfortune's burdens is, that as soon as a charge is fastened upon the unhappy, they are believed to have deserved their sufferings. I, for my part, who have been banished from all life's blessings, stripped of my honours, stained in repute, am punished for well-doing.

'And now methinks I see the villainous dens of the wicked surging with joy and gladness, all the most recklessly unscrupulous threatening a new crop of lying informations, the good prostrate with terror at my danger, every ruffian incited by impunity to new daring and to success by the profits of audacity, the guiltless not only robbed of their peace of mind, but even of all means of defence. Wherefore I would fain cry out :

SONG V.

BOETHIUS' PRAYER.

'Builder of yon starry dome,
  Thou that whirlest, throned eternal,
Heaven's swift globe, and, as they roam,
  Guid'st the stars by laws supernal :

So in full-sphered splendour dight
Cynthia dims the lamps of night,
But unto the orb fraternal
Closer drawn,* doth lose her light.

'Who at fall of eventide,
Hesper, his cold radiance showeth,
Lucifer his beams doth hide,
Paling as the sun's light groweth,
Brief, while winter's frost holds sway,
By thy will the space of day;
Swift, when summer's fervour gloweth,
Speed the hours of night away.

'Thou dost rule the changing year:
When rude Boreas oppresses,
Fall the leaves; they reappear,
Wooed by Zephyr's soft caresses.
Fields that Sirius burns deep-grown
By Arcturus' watch were sown:
Each the reign of law confesses,
Keeps the place that is his own.

* The moon is regarded as farthest from the sun at the full, and, as she wanes, approaching gradually nearer.

'Sovereign Ruler, Lord of all!
Can it be that Thou disdainest
Only man? 'Gainst him, poor thrall,
Wanton Fortune plays her vainest.
Guilt's deservèd punishment
Falleth on the innocent;
High uplifted, the profanest
On the just their malice vent.

'Virtue cowers in dark retreats,
Crime's foul stain the righteous beareth,
Perjury and false deceits
Hurt not him the wrong who dareth;
But whene'er the wicked trust
In ill strength to work their lust,
Kings, whom nations' awe declareth
Mighty, grovel in the dust.

'Look, oh look upon this earth,
Thou who on law's sure foundation
Framedst all! Have we no worth,
We poor men, of all creation?
Sore we toss on fortune's tide;
Master, bid the waves subside!
And earth's ways with consummation
Of Thy heaven's order guide!'

V.

When I had poured out my griefs in this long and unbroken strain of lamentation, she, with calm countenance, and in no wise disturbed at my complainings, thus spake:

'When I saw thee sorrowful, in tears, I straightway knew thee wretched and an exile. But how far distant that exile I should not know, had not thine own speech revealed it. Yet how far indeed from thy country hast thou, not been banished, but rather hast strayed; or, if thou wilt have it banishment, hast banished thyself! For no one else could ever lawfully have had this power over thee. Now, if thou wilt call to mind from what country thou art sprung, it is not ruled, as once was the Athenian polity, by the sovereignty of the multitude, but "one is its Ruler, one its King," who takes delight in the number of His citizens, not in their banishment ; to submit to whose governance and to obey whose ordinances is perfect freedom. Art thou ignorant of that most ancient law of this thy country, whereby it is decreed that no one whatsoever, who hath chosen to fix there his dwelling, may be sent into exile? For truly there is no fear that one who is encompassed by its ramparts and defences should deserve to be exiled. But he who has ceased to wish to dwell therein, he likewise ceases to deserve to do so. And so it is not so much the aspect of this place which moves me, as thy aspect ; not so much the library walls set off with glass and ivory which I miss, as the chamber of thy mind, wherein I once placed, not books, but that which gives books their value, the doctrines which my books contain. Now, what thou hast said of thy services to the commonweal is true, only too little compared with the greatness of thy deservings. The things laid to thy charge whereof thou hast spoken, whether such as redound to thy credit, or mere false accusations, are publicly known. As for the crimes and deceits of the informers, thou hast rightly deemed it fitting to pass them over lightly, because the popular voice hath better and more fully pronounced upon them. Thou hast bitterly complained of the injustice of the senate. Thou hast grieved over my calumniation, and likewise hast lamented the damage to my good name. Finally, thine indignation blazed forth against fortune ; thou hast complained of the unfairness with which thy merits have been recompensed. Last of all thy frantic muse framed a prayer that the peace which reigns in heaven might rule earth also. But since a throng of tumultuous passions hath assailed thy soul, since thou art distraught with anger, pain, and grief, strong remedies are not proper for thee in this thy present mood. And so for a time I will use milder methods, that the tumours which have grown hard through the influx of disturbing passion may be softened by gentle treatment, till they can bear the force of sharper remedies.'

SONG VI.

All Things have their Needful Order.

He who to th' unwilling furrows
  Gives the generous grain,
When the Crab with baleful fervours
  Scorches all the plain;
He shall find his garner bare,
Acorns for his scanty fare.

Go not forth to cull sweet violets
  From the purpled steep,
While the furious blasts of winter
  Through the valleys sweep;
Nor the grape o'erhasty bring
To the press in days of spring.

For to each thing God hath given
  Its appointed time;
No perplexing change permits He
  In His plan sublime.
So who quits the order due
Shall a luckless issue rue.

VI.

'First, then, wilt thou suffer me by a few questions to make some attempt to test the state of thy mind, that I may learn in what way to set about thy cure?'

'Ask what thou wilt,' said I, 'for I will answer whatever questions thou choosest to put.'

Then said she: 'This world of ours—thinkest thou it is governed haphazard and fortuitously, or believest thou that there is in it any rational guidance?'

'Nay,' said I, 'in no wise may I deem that such fixed motions can be determined by random hazard, but I know that God, the Creator, presideth over His work, nor will the day ever come that shall drive me from holding fast the truth of this belief.'

'Yes,' said she; 'thou didst even but now affirm it in song, lamenting that men alone had no portion in the divine care. As to the rest, thou wert unshaken in the belief that they were ruled by reason. Yet I marvel exceedingly how, in spite of thy firm hold on this opinion, thou art fallen into sickness. But let us probe more deeply: something or other is missing, I think. Now, tell me, since thou doubtest not that God governs the world, dost thou perceive by what means He rules it?'

'I scarcely understand what thou meanest,' I said, 'much less can I answer thy question.'

'Did I not say truly that something is missing, whereby, as through a breach in the ramparts, disease hath crept in to disturb thy mind? But, tell me, dost thou remember the universal end towards which the aim of all nature is directed?'

'I once heard,' said I, 'but sorrow hath dulled my recollection.'

'And yet thou knowest whence all things have proceeded.'

'Yes, that I know,' said I, 'and have answered that it is from God.'

'Yet how is it possible that thou knowest not what is the end of existence, when thou dost understand its source and origin?

However, these disturbances of mind have force to shake a man's position, but cannot pluck him up and root him altogether out of himself. But answer this also, I pray thee: rememberest thou that thou art a man?'

'How should I not?' said I.

'Then, canst thou say what man is?'

'Is this thy question: Whether I know myself for a being endowed with reason and subject to death? Surely I do acknowledge myself such.'

Then she: 'Dost know nothing else that thou art?'

'Nothing.'

'Now,' said she, 'I know another cause of thy disease, one, too, of grave moment. Thou hast ceased to know thy own nature. So, then, I have made full discovery both of the causes of thy sickness and the means of restoring thy health. It is because forgetfulness of thyself hath bewildered thy mind that thou hast bewailed thee as an exile, as one stripped of the blessings that were his; it is because thou knowest not the end of existence that thou deemest abominable and wicked men to be happy and powerful; while, because thou hast forgotten by what means the earth is governed, thou deemest that fortune's changes ebb and flow without the restraint of a guiding hand. These are serious enough to cause not sickness only, but even death; but, thanks be to the Author of our health, the light of nature hath not yet left thee utterly. In thy true judgment concerning the world's government, in that thou believest it subject, not to the random drift of chance, but to divine reason, we have the divine spark from which thy recovery may be hoped. Have, then, no fear; from these weak embers the vital heat shall once more be kindled within thee. But seeing that it is not yet time for strong remedies, and that the mind is manifestly so constituted that when it casts off true opinions it straightway puts on false, wherefrom arises a cloud of confusion that disturbs its true vision, I will now try and disperse these mists by mild and soothing application, that so the darkness of misleading passion may be scattered, and thou mayst come to discern the splendour of the true light.'

SONG VII.

The Perturbations of Passion.

Stars shed no light
  Through the black night,
    When the clouds hide;
And the lashed wave,
  If the winds rave
    O'er ocean's tide,—

Though once serene
  As day's fair sheen,—
    Soon fouled and spoiled
By the storm's spite,
  Shows to the sight
    Turbid and soiled.

Oft the fair rill,
  Down the steep hill
    Seaward that strays,
Some tumbled block
  Of fallen rock
    Hinders and stays.

Then art thou fain
   Clear and most plain
      Truth to discern,
In the right way
   Firmly to stay,
      Nor from it turn?

Joy, hope and fear
   Suffer not near,
      Drive grief away:
Shackled and blind
   And lost is the mind
      Where these have sway.

BOOK II.

THE VANITY OF FORTUNE'S GIFTS.

SUMMARY.

CH. I. Philosophy reproves Boethius for the foolishness of his complaints against Fortune. Her very nature is caprice.—CH. II. Philosophy in Fortune's name replies to Boethius' reproaches, and proves that the gifts of Fortune are hers to give and to take away.—CH. III. Boethius falls back upon his present sense of misery. Philosophy reminds him of the brilliancy of his former fortunes.—CH. IV. Boethius objects that the memory of past happiness is the bitterest portion of the lot of the unhappy. Philosophy shows that much is still left for which he may be thankful. None enjoy perfect satisfaction with their lot. But happiness depends not on anything which Fortune can give. It is to be sought within.—CH. V. All the gifts of

Fortune are external; they can never truly be our own. Man cannot find his good in worldly possessions. Riches bring anxiety and trouble.—CH. VI. High place without virtue is an evil, not a good. Power is an empty name.—CH. VII. Fame is a thing of little account when compared with the immensity of the Universe and the endlessness of Time.—CH. VIII. One service only can Fortune do, when she reveals her own nature and distinguishes true friends from false.

BOOK II.

I.

THEREAFTER for awhile she remained silent; and when she had restored my flagging attention by a moderate pause in her discourse, she thus began: 'If I have thoroughly ascertained the character and causes of thy sickness, thou art pining with regretful longing for thy former fortune. It is the change, as thou deemest, of this fortune that hath so wrought upon thy mind. Well do I understand that Siren's manifold wiles, the fatal charm of the friendship she pretends for her victims, so long as she is scheming to entrap them—how she unexpectedly abandons them and leaves them overwhelmed with insupportable grief. Bethink thee of her nature, character, and deserts, and thou wilt soon acknowledge that in her thou hast neither possessed, nor hast thou lost, aught of any worth. Methinks I need not spend much pains in bringing this to thy mind, since, even when she was still with thee, even while she was caressing thee, thou usedst to assail her in manly terms, to rebuke her, with maxims drawn from my holy treasure-house. But all sudden changes of circumstances bring inevitably a certain commotion of spirit. Thus it hath come to pass that thou also for awhile hast been parted from thy mind's tranquillity. But it is time for thee to take and drain a draught, soft and pleasant to the taste, which, as it penetrates within, may prepare the way for stronger potions. Wherefore I call to my aid the sweet persuasiveness of Rhetoric, who then only walketh in the right way when she forsakes not my instructions, and Music, my handmaid, I bid to join with her singing, now in lighter, now in graver strain.

'What is it, then, poor mortal, that hath cast thee into lamentation and mourning?

Some strange, unwonted sight, methinks, have thine eyes seen. Thou deemest Fortune to have changed towards thee; thou mistakest. Such ever were her ways, ever such her nature. Rather in her very mutability hath she preserved towards thee her true constancy. Such was she when she loaded thee with caresses, when she deluded thee with the allurements of a false happiness. Thou hast found out how changeful is the face of the blind goddess. She who still veils herself from others hath fully discovered to thee her whole character. If thou likest her, take her as she is, and do not complain. If thou abhorrest her perfidy, turn from her in disdain, renounce her, for baneful are her delusions. The very thing which is now the cause of thy great grief ought to have brought thee tranquillity. Thou hast been forsaken by one of whom no one can be sure that she will not forsake him. Or dost thou indeed set value on a happiness that is certain to depart? Again I ask, Is Fortune's presence dear to thee if she cannot be trusted to stay, and though she will bring sorrow when she is gone?

Why, if she cannot be kept at pleasure, and if her flight overwhelms with calamity, what is this fleeting visitant but a token of coming trouble? Truly it is not enough to look only at what lies before the eyes; wisdom gauges the issues of things, and this same mutability, with its two aspects, makes the threats of Fortune void of terror, and her caresses little to be desired. Finally, thou oughtest to bear with whatever takes place within the boundaries of Fortune's demesne, when thou hast placed thy head beneath her yoke. But if thou wishest to impose a law of staying and departing on her whom thou hast of thine own accord chosen for thy mistress, art thou not acting wrongfully, art thou not embittering by impatience a lot which thou canst not alter? Didst thou commit thy sails to the winds, thou wouldst voyage not whither thy intention was to go, but whither the winds drave thee; didst thou entrust thy seed to the fields, thou wouldst set off the fruitful years against the barren. Thou hast resigned thyself to the sway of Fortune; thou must submit to thy mistress's caprices. What! art thou verily striving to stay the swing of the revolving wheel? Oh, stupidest of mortals, if it takes to standing still, it ceases to be the wheel of Fortune.'

SONG I.

Fortune's Malice.

Mad Fortune sweeps along in wanton pride,
Uncertain as Euripus' surging tide;
Now tramples mighty kings beneath her feet;
Now sets the conquered in the victor's seat.
She heedeth not the wail of hapless woe,
But mocks the griefs that from her mischief flow.
Such is her sport; so proveth she her power;
And great the marvel, when in one brief hour
She shows her darling lifted high in bliss,
Then headlong plunged in misery's abyss.

II.

'Now I would fain also reason with thee a little in Fortune's own words. Do thou observe whether her contentions be just. "Man," she might say, "why dost thou pursue me with thy daily complainings? What wrong have I done thee? What goods of thine have I taken from thee? Choose an thou wilt a judge, and let us dispute before him concerning the rightful ownership of wealth and rank. If thou succeedest in showing that any one of these things is the true property of mortal man, I freely grant those things to be thine which thou claimest. When nature brought thee forth out of thy mother's womb, I took thee, naked and destitute as thou wast, I cherished thee with my substance, and, in the partiality of my favour for thee, I brought thee up somewhat too indulgently, and this it is which now makes thee rebellious against me. I surrounded thee with a royal abundance of all those things that are in my power. Now it is my pleasure to draw back my hand. Thou hast reason to thank me for the use of what was not thine own; thou hast no right to complain, as if thou hadst lost what was wholly thine. Why, then, dost bemoan thyself? I have done thee no violence. Wealth, honour, and all such things are placed under my control. My handmaidens know their mistress; with me they come, and at my going they depart. I might boldly affirm that if those things the loss of which thou lamentest had been thine, thou couldst never have lost them. Am I alone to be forbidden to do what I will with my own? Unrebuked, the skies now reveal the brightness of day, now shroud the daylight in the darkness of night; the year may now engarland the face of the earth with flowers and fruits, now disfigure it with storms and cold. The sea is permitted to invite with smooth and tranquil surface to-day, tomorrow to roughen with wave and storm. Shall man's insatiate greed bind *me* to a constancy foreign to my character? This is my art, this the game I never cease to play. I turn the wheel that spins. I delight to see the high come down and the low ascend. Mount up, if thou wilt, but only on condition that thou wilt not think it a hardship to come down when the rules of my game require it. Wert thou ignorant of my character? Didst not know how Crœsus, King of the Lydians, erstwhile the dreaded rival of Cyrus, was afterwards pitiably consigned to the flame of the pyre, and only saved by a shower sent from heaven? Has it 'scaped thee how Paullus paid a meed of pious tears to the misfortunes of King Perseus, his prisoner? What else do tragedies make such woeful outcry over save the overthrow of kingdoms by the indiscriminate strokes of Fortune? Didst thou not learn in thy childhood how there stand at the threshold of Zeus 'two jars,' 'the one full of blessings, the other of calamities'? How if thou hast drawn over-liberally from the good jar? What if not even now have I departed wholly from thee? What if this very mutability of mine is a just ground for hoping better things? But listen now, and cease to let thy heart consume away with fretfulness, nor expect to live on thine own terms in a realm that is common to all.'

SONG II.

MAN'S COVETOUSNESS.

What though Plenty pour her gifts
  With a lavish hand,
Numberless as are the stars,
  Countless as the sand,
Will the race of man, content,
Cease to murmur and lament?

Nay, though God, all-bounteous, give
  Gold at man's desire—
Honours, rank, and fame—content
  Not a whit is nigher;
But an all-devouring greed
Yawns with ever-widening need.

Then what bounds can e'er restrain
  This wild lust of having,
When with each new bounty fed
  Grows the frantic craving?
He is never rich whose fear
Sees grim Want forever near.

III.

'If Fortune should plead thus against thee, assuredly thou wouldst not have one word to offer in reply; or, if thou canst find any justification of thy complainings, thou must show what it is. I will give thee space to speak.'

Then said I: 'Verily, thy pleas are plausible—yea, steeped in the honeyed sweetness of music and rhetoric. But their charm lasts only while they are sounding in the ear; the sense of his misfortunes lies deeper in the heart of the wretched. So, when the sound ceases to vibrate upon the air, the heart's indwelling sorrow is felt with renewed bitterness.'

Then said she: 'It is indeed as thou sayest, for we have not yet come to the curing of thy sickness; as yet these are but lenitives conducing to the treatment of a malady hitherto obstinate. The remedies which go deep I will apply in due season. Nevertheless, to deprecate thy determination to be thought wretched, I ask thee, Hast thou forgotten the extent and bounds of thy felicity? I say nothing of how, when orphaned and desolate, thou wast taken into the care of illustrious men; how thou wast chosen for alliance with the highest in the state—and even before thou wert bound to their house by marriage, wert already dear to their love—which is the most precious of all ties. Did not all pronounce thee most happy in the virtues of thy wife, the splendid honours of her father, and the blessing of male issue? I pass over—for I care not to speak of blessings in which others also have shared—the distinctions often denied to age which thou enjoyedst in thy youth. I choose rather to come to the unparalleled culmination of thy good fortune. If the fruition of any earthly success has weight in the scale of happiness, can the memory of that splendour be swept away by any rising flood of troubles? That day when thou didst see thy two sons ride forth from home joint consuls, followed by a train of senators, and welcomed by the good-will of the people; when these two sat in curule chairs in the Senate-house, and thou by thy panegyric on the king didst earn the fame of eloquence and ability; when in the Circus, seated between the two consuls, thou didst glut the multitude thronging around with the triumphal largesses for which they looked—methinks thou didst cozen Fortune while she caressed thee, and made thee her darling. Thou didst bear off a boon which she had never before granted to any private person. Art thou, then, minded to cast up a reckoning with Fortune? Now for the first time she has turned a jealous glance upon thee. If thou compare the extent and bounds of thy blessings and misfortunes, thou canst not deny that thou art still fortunate. Or if thou esteem not thyself favoured by Fortune in that thy then seeming prosperity hath departed, deem not thyself wretched, since what thou now believest to be calamitous passeth also. What! art thou but now come suddenly and a stranger to the scene of this life? Thinkest thou there is any stability in human affairs, when man himself vanishes away in the swift course of time? It is true that there is little trust that the gifts of chance will abide; yet the last day of life is in a manner the death of all remaining Fortune. What difference, then, thinkest thou, is there, whether thou leavest her by dying, or she leave thee by fleeing away?'

SONG III.

ALL PASSES.

When, in rosy chariot drawn,
Phœbus 'gins to light the dawn,
By his flaming beams assailed,
Every glimmering star is paled.
When the grove, by Zephyrs fed,
With rose-blossom blushes red;—
Doth rude Auster breathe thereon,
Bare it stands, its glory gone.
Smooth and tranquil lies the deep
While the winds are hushed in sleep.
Soon, when angry tempests lash,
Wild and high the billows dash.
Thus if Nature's changing face
Holds not still a moment's space,
Fleeting deem man's fortunes; deem
Bliss as transient as a dream.
One law only standeth fast:
Things created may not last.

IV.

Then said I: 'True are thine admonishings, thou nurse of all excellence; nor can I deny the wonder of my fortune's swift career. Yet it is this which chafes me the more cruelly in the recalling. For truly in adverse fortune the worst sting of misery is to *have been* happy.'

'Well,' said she, 'if thou art paying the penalty of a mistaken belief, thou canst not rightly impute the fault to circumstances. If it is the felicity which Fortune gives that moves thee—mere name though it be—come reckon up with me how rich thou art in the number and weightiness of thy blessings. Then if, by the blessing of Providence, thou hast still preserved unto thee safe and inviolate that which, howsoever thou mightest reckon thy fortune, thou wouldst have thought thy most precious possession, what right hast thou to talk of ill-fortune whilst keeping all

Fortune's better gifts? Yet Symmachus, thy wife's father—a man whose splendid character does honour to the human race—is safe and unharmed; and while he bewails thy wrongs, this rare nature, in whom wisdom and virtue are so nobly blended, is himself out of danger—a boon thou wouldst have been quick to purchase at the price of life itself. Thy wife yet lives, with her gentle disposition, her peerless modesty and virtue—this the epitome of all her graces, that she is the true daughter of her sire—she lives, I say, and for thy sake only preserves the breath of life, though she loathes it, and pines away in grief and tears for thy absence, wherein, if in naught else, I would allow some marring of thy felicity. What shall I say of thy sons and their consular dignity—how in them, so far as may be in youths of their age, the example of their father's and grandfather's character shines out? Since, then, the chief care of mortal man is to preserve his life, how happy art thou, couldst thou but recognise thy blessings, who possessest even now what no one doubts to be dearer than life! Wherefore, now dry thy tears. Fortune's hate hath not involved all thy dear ones; the stress of the storm that has assailed thee is not beyond measure intolerable, since there are anchors still holding firm which suffer thee not to lack either consolation in the present or hope for the future.'

'I pray that they still may hold. For while they still remain, however things may go, I shall ride out the storm. Yet thou seest how much is shorn of the splendour of my fortunes.'

'We are gaining a little ground,' said she, 'if there is something in thy lot wherewith thou art not yet altogether discontented. But I cannot stomach thy daintiness when thou complainest with such violence of grief and anxiety because thy happiness falls short of completeness. Why, who enjoys such settled felicity as not to have some quarrel with the circumstances of his lot? A troublous matter are the conditions of human bliss; either they are never realized in full, or never stay permanently. One has abundant riches, but is shamed by his ignoble birth. Another is conspicuous for his nobility, but through the embarrassments of poverty would prefer to be obscure. A third, richly endowed with both, laments the loneliness of an unwedded life. Another, though happily married, is doomed to childlessness, and nurses his wealth for a stranger to inherit. Yet another, blest with children, mournfully bewails the misdeeds of son or daughter. Wherefore, it is not easy for anyone to be at perfect peace with the circumstances of his lot. There lurks in each several portion something which they who experience it not know nothing of, but which makes the sufferer wince. Besides, the more favoured a man is by Fortune, the more fastidiously sensitive is he ; and, unless all things answer to his whim, he is overwhelmed by the most trifling misfortunes, because utterly unschooled in adversity. So petty are the trifles which rob the most fortunate of perfect happiness ! How many are there, dost thou imagine, who would think themselves nigh heaven, if but a small portion from the wreck of thy fortune should fall to them? This very place which thou callest exile is to them that dwell therein their native land. So true is it that nothing is wretched, but thinking makes it so, and conversely every lot is happy if borne with equanimity. Who is so blest by Fortune as not to wish to change his state, if once he gives rein to a rebellious spirit? With how many bitternesses is the sweetness of human felicity blent! And even if that sweetness seem to him to bring delight in the enjoying, yet he cannot keep it from departing when it will. How manifestly wretched, then, is the bliss of earthly fortune, which lasts not for ever with those whose temper is equable, and can give no perfect satisfaction to the anxious-minded!

'Why, then, ye children of mortality, seek ye from without that happiness whose seat is only within us? Error and ignorance bewilder you. I will show thee, in brief, the hinge on which perfect happiness turns. Is there anything more precious to thee than thyself? Nothing, thou wilt say. If, then, thou art master of thyself, thou wilt possess that which thou wilt never be willing to lose, and which Fortune cannot take from thee. And that thou mayst see that happiness cannot possibly consist in these things which are the sport of chance, reflect that, if happiness is the highest good of a creature living in accordance with reason, and if a thing which can in any wise be reft away is not the highest good, since that which cannot be taken away is better than it, it is plain that Fortune cannot aspire to bestow happiness by reason of its instability. And, besides, a man borne along by this transitory felicity must either know or not know its unstability. If he knows not, how poor is a happiness which depends on the blindness of ignorance! If he knows it, he needs must fear to lose a happiness whose loss he believes to be possible. Wherefore, a never-ceasing fear suffers him not to be happy. Or does he count the possibility of this loss a trifling matter? Insignificant, then, must be the good whose loss can be borne so equably. And, further, I know thee to be one settled in the belief that the souls of men certainly die not with them, and convinced thereof by numerous proofs; it is clear also that the felicity which Fortune bestows is brought to an end with the death of the body: therefore, it cannot be doubted but that, if happiness is conferred in this way, the whole human race sinks into misery when death brings the close of all. But if we know that many have sought the joy of happiness not through death only, but also through pain and suffering, how can life make men happy by its presence when it makes them not wretched by its loss?'

SONG IV.

THE GOLDEN MEAN.

Who founded firm and sure
Would ever live secure,
In spite of storm and blast
Immovable and fast;
Whoso would fain deride
The ocean's threatening tide;—
His dwelling should not seek
On sands or mountain-peak.
Upon the mountain's height
The storm-winds wreak their spite:
The shifting sands disdain
Their burden to sustain.

Do thou these perils flee,
Fair though the prospect be,
And fix thy resting-place
On some low rock's sure base.
Then, though the tempests roar,
Seas thunder on the shore,
Thou in thy stronghold blest
And undisturbed shalt rest;
Live all thy days serene,
And mock the heavens' spleen.

V.

'But since my reasonings begin to work a soothing effect within thy mind, methinks I may resort to remedies somewhat stronger. Come, suppose, now, the gifts of Fortune were not fleeting and transitory, what is there in them capable of ever becoming truly thine, or which does not lose value when looked at steadily and fairly weighed in the balance? Are riches, I pray thee, precious either through thy nature or in their own? What are they but mere gold and heaps of money? Yet these fine things show their quality better in the spending than in the hoarding; for I suppose 'tis plain that greed always makes men hateful, while liberality brings fame. But that which is transferred to another cannot remain in one's own possession; and if that be so, then money is only precious when it is given away, and, by being transferred to others, ceases to be one's own. Again, if all the money in the world were heaped up in one man's possession, all others would be made poor. Sound fills the ears of many at the same time without being broken into parts, but your riches cannot pass to many without being lessened in the process. And when this happens, they must needs impoverish those whom they leave. How poor and cramped a thing, then, is riches, which more than one cannot possess as an unbroken whole, which falls not to any one man's lot without the impoverishment of everyone else! Or is it the glitter of gems that allures the eye? Yet, how rarely excellent soever may be their splendour, remember the flashing light is in the jewels, not in the man. Indeed, I greatly marvel at men's admiration of them; for what can rightly seem beautiful to a being endowed with life and reason, if it lack the movement and structure of life? And although such things do in the end take on them more beauty from their Maker's care and their own brilliancy, still they in no wise merit your admiration since their excellence is set at a lower grade than your own.

'Does the beauty of the fields delight you? Surely, yes; it is a beautiful part of a right beautiful whole. Fitly indeed do we at times enjoy the serene calm of the sea, admire the sky, the stars, the moon, the sun. Yet is any of these thy concern? Dost thou venture to boast thyself of the beauty of any one of them? Art *thou* decked with spring's flowers? is it *thy* fertility that swelleth in the fruits of autumn? Why art thou moved with empty transports? why embracest thou an alien excellence as thine own? Never will fortune make thine that which the nature of things has excluded from thy ownership. Doubtless the fruits of the earth are given for the sustenance of living creatures. But if thou art content to supply thy wants so far as suffices nature, there is no need to resort to fortune's bounty. Nature is content with few things, and with a very little of these. If thou art minded to force superfluities upon her when she is satisfied, that which thou addest will prove either unpleasant or harmful. But, now, thou thinkest it fine to shine in raiment of divers colours; yet—if, indeed, there is any pleasure in the sight of such things—it is the texture or the artist's skill which I shall admire.

'Or perhaps it is a long train of servants that makes thee happy? Why, if they behave viciously, they are a ruinous burden to thy house, and exceeding dangerous to their own master; while if they are honest, how canst thou count other men's virtue in the sum of thy possessions? From all which 'tis plainly proved that not one of these things which thou reckonest in the number of thy possessions is really thine. And if there is in them no beauty to be desired, why shouldst thou either grieve for their loss or find joy in their continued possession? While if they are beautiful in their own nature, what is that to thee? They would have been not less pleasing in themselves, though never included among thy possessions. For they derive not their preciousness from being counted in thy riches, but rather thou hast chosen to count them in thy riches because they seemed to thee precious.

'Then, what seek ye by all this noisy outcry about fortune? To chase away poverty, I ween, by means of abundance. And yet ye find the result just contrary. Why, this varied array of precious furniture needs more accessories for its protection; it is a true saying that they want most who possess most, and, conversely, they want very little who measure their abundance by nature's requirements, not by the superfluity of vain display. Have ye no good of your own implanted within you, that ye seek your good in things external and separate? Is the nature of things so reversed that a creature divine by right of reason can in no other way be splendid in his own eyes save by the possession of lifeless chattels? Yet, while other things are content with their own, ye who in your intellect are God-like seek from the lowest of things adornment for a nature of supreme excellence, and perceive not how great a wrong ye do your Maker. His will was that mankind should excel all things on earth. Ye thrust down your worth beneath the lowest of things. For if that in which each thing finds its good is plainly more precious than that whose good it is, by your own estimation ye put yourselves below the vilest of things, when ye deem these vile things to be your good: nor does this fall out undeservedly. Indeed, man is so constituted that he then only excels other things when he knows himself; but he is brought lower than the beasts if he lose this self-knowledge. For that other creatures should be ignorant of themselves is natural; in man it shows as a defect. How extravagant, then, is this error of yours, in thinking that anything can be embellished by adornments not its own. It cannot be. For if such accessories add any lustre, it is the accessories that get the praise, while that which they veil and cover remains in its pristine ugliness. And again I say, That is no *good*, which injures its possessor. Is this untrue? No, quite true, thou sayest. And yet riches have often hurt those that possessed them, since the worst of men, who are all the more covetous by reason of their wickedness, think none but themselves worthy to possess all the gold and gems the world contains. So thou, who now dreadest pike and sword, mightest have trolled a carol "in the robber's face," hadst thou entered the road of life with empty pockets. Oh, wondrous blessedness of perishable wealth, whose acquisition robs thee of security!'

SONG V.

THE FORMER AGE.

Too blest the former age, their life
  Who in the fields contented led,
And still, by luxury unspoiled,
  On frugal acorns sparely fed.

No skill was theirs the luscious grape
  With honey's sweetness to confuse;
Nor China's soft and sheeny silks
  T' empurple with brave Tyrian hues.

The grass their wholesome couch, their drink
  The stream, their roof the pine's tall shade;
Not theirs to cleave the deep, nor seek
  In strange far lands the spoils of trade.

The trump of war was heard not yet,
  Nor soiled the fields by bloodshed's
    stain ;
For why should war's fierce madness arm
  When strife brought wound, but brought
    not gain ?

Ah ! would our hearts might still return
  To following in those ancient ways.
Alas ! the greed of getting glows
  More fierce than Etna's fiery blaze.

Woe, woe for him, whoe'er it was,
  Who first gold's hidden store revealed,
And—perilous treasure-trove—dug out
  The gems that fain would be concealed !

VI.

'What now shall I say of rank and power, whereby, because ye know not true power and dignity, ye hope to reach the sky? Yet, when rank and power have fallen to the worst of men, did ever an Etna, belching forth flame and fiery deluge, work such mischief? Verily, as I think, thou dost remember how thine ancestors sought to abolish the consular power, which had been the foundation of their liberties, on account of the overweening pride of the consuls, and how for that self-same pride they had already abolished the kingly title! And if, as happens but rarely, these prerogatives are conferred on virtuous men, it is only the virtue of those who exercise them that pleases. So it appears that honour cometh not to virtue from rank, but to rank from virtue. Look, too, at the nature of that power which ye find so attractive and glorious! Do ye never consider, ye creatures of earth, what ye are, and over whom ye exercise your fancied lordship? Suppose, now, that in the mouse tribe there should rise up one claiming rights and powers for himself above the rest, would ye not laugh consumedly? Yet if thou lookest to his body alone, what creature canst thou find more feeble than man, who oftentimes is killed by the bite of a fly, or by some insect creeping into the inner passage of his system! Yet what rights can one exercise over another, save only as regards the body, and that which is lower than the body—I mean fortune? What! wilt thou bind with thy mandates the free spirit? Canst thou force from its due tranquillity the mind that is firmly composed by reason? A tyrant thought to drive a man of free birth to reveal his accomplices in a conspiracy, but the prisoner bit off his tongue and threw it into the furious tyrant's face; thus, the tortures which the tyrant thought the instrument of his cruelty the sage made an opportunity for heroism. Moreover, what is there that one man can do to another which he himself may not have to undergo in his turn? We are told that Busiris, who used to kill his guests, was himself slain by his guest, Hercules. Regulus had thrown into bonds many of the Carthaginians whom he had taken in war; soon after he himself submitted his hands to the chains of the vanquished. Then, thinkest thou that man hath any power who cannot prevent another's being able to do to him what he himself can do to others?

'Besides, if there were any element of natural and proper good in rank and power, they would never come to the utterly bad, since opposites are not wont to be associated. Nature brooks not the union of contraries. So, seeing there is no doubt that wicked wretches are oftentimes set in high places, it is also clear that things which suffer association with the worst of men cannot be good in their own nature. Indeed, this judgment may with some reason be passed concerning all the gifts of fortune which fall so plentifully to all the most wicked. This ought also to be considered here, I think: No one doubts a man to be brave in whom he has observed a brave spirit residing. It is plain that one who is endowed with speed is swift-footed. So also music makes men musical, the healing art physicians, rhetoric public speakers. For each of these has naturally its own proper working; there is no confusion with the effects of contrary things—nay, even of itself it rejects what is incompatible. And yet wealth cannot extinguish insatiable greed, nor has power ever made him master of himself whom vicious lusts kept bound in indissoluble fetters; dignity conferred on the wicked not only fails to make them worthy, but contrarily reveals and displays their unworthiness. Why does it so happen? Because ye take pleasure in calling by false names things whose nature is quite incongruous thereto—by names which are easily proved false by the very effects of the things themselves; even so it is; these riches, that power, this dignity, are none of them rightly so called. Finally, we may draw the same conclusion concerning the whole sphere of Fortune, within which there is plainly nothing to be truly desired, nothing of intrinsic excellence; for she neither always joins herself to the good, nor does she make good men of those to whom she is united.'

SONG VI.

NERO'S INFAMY.

We know what mischief dire he wrought—
  Rome fired, the Fathers slain—
Whose hand with brother's slaughter wet
  A mother's blood did stain.

No pitying tear his cheek bedewed,
  As on the corse he gazed;
That mother's beauty, once so fair,
  A critic's voice appraised.

Yet far and wide, from East to West,
  His sway the nations own;
And scorching South and icy North
  Obey his will alone.

Did, then, high power a curb impose
  On Nero's phrenzied will?
Ah, woe when to the evil heart
  Is joined the sword to kill!

VII.

Then said I: 'Thou knowest thyself that ambition for worldly success hath but little swayed me. Yet I have desired opportunity for action, lest virtue, in default of exercise, should languish away.'

Then she: 'This is that "last infirmity" which is able to allure minds which, though of noble quality, have not yet been moulded to any exquisite refinement by the perfecting of the virtues—I mean, the love of glory—and fame for high services rendered to the commonweal. And yet consider with me how poor and unsubstantial a thing this glory is! The whole of this earth's globe, as thou hast learnt from the demonstration of astronomy, compared with the expanse of heaven, is found no bigger than a point; that is to say, if measured by the vastness of heaven's sphere, it is held to occupy absolutely no space at all. Now, of this so insignificant portion of the universe, it is about a fourth part, as Ptolemy's proofs have taught us, which is inhabited by living creatures known to us. If from this fourth part you take away in thought all that is usurped by seas and marshes, or lies a vast waste of waterless desert, barely is an exceeding narrow area left for human habitation. You, then, who are shut in and prisoned in this merest fraction of a point's space, do ye take thought for the blazoning of your fame, for the spreading abroad of your renown? Why, what amplitude or magnificence has glory when confined to such narrow and petty limits?

'Besides, the straitened bounds of this scant dwelling-place are inhabited by many nations differing widely in speech, in usages, in mode of life; to many of these, from the difficulty of travel, from diversities of speech, from want of commercial intercourse, the fame not only of individual men, but even of cities, is unable to reach. Why, in Cicero's days, as he himself somewhere points out, the fame of the Roman Republic had not yet crossed the Caucasus, and yet by that time her name had grown formidable to the Parthians and other nations of those parts. Seest thou, then, how narrow, how confined, is the glory ye take pains to spread abroad and extend! Can the fame of a single Roman penetrate where the glory of the Roman name fails to pass? Moreover, the customs and institutions of different races agree not together, so that what is deemed praiseworthy in one country is thought punishable in another. Wherefore, if any love the applause of fame, it shall not profit him to publish his name among many peoples. Then, each must be content to have the range of his glory limited to his own people; the splendid immortality of fame must be confined within the bounds of a single race.

'Once more, how many of high renown in their own times have been lost in oblivion for want of a record! Indeed, of what avail are written records even, which, with their authors, are overtaken by the dimness of age after a somewhat longer time? But ye, when ye think on future fame, fancy it an immortality that ye are begetting for yourselves. Why, if thou scannest the infinite spaces of eternity, what room hast thou left for rejoicing in the durability of thy name? Verily, if a single moment's space be compared with ten thousand years, it has a certain relative duration, however little, since each period is definite. But this same number of years—ay, and a number many times as great—cannot even be compared with endless duration; for, indeed, finite periods may in a sort be compared one with another, but a finite and an infinite never. So it comes to pass that fame, though it extend to ever so wide a space of years, if it be compared to never-lessening eternity, seems not short-lived merely, but altogether nothing. But as for you, ye know not how to act aright, unless it be to court the popular breeze, and win the empty applause of the multitude—nay, ye abandon the superlative worth of conscience and virtue, and ask a recompense from the poor words of others. Let me tell thee how wittily one did mock the shallowness of this sort of arrogance. A certain man assailed one who had put on the name of philosopher as a cloak to pride and vain-glory, not for the practice of real virtue, and added: "Now shall I know if thou art a philosopher if thou bearest reproaches calmly and patiently." The other for awhile affected to be patient, and, having endured to be abused, cried out derisively: "*Now*, do you see that I am a philosopher?" The other, with biting sarcasm, retorted: "I should have hadst thou held thy peace." Moreover, what concern have choice spirits—for it is of such men we speak, men who seek glory by virtue—what concern, I say, have these with fame after the dissolution of the body in death's last hour? For if men die wholly—which our reasonings forbid us to believe—there is no such thing as glory at all, since he to whom the glory is said to belong is altogether non-existent. But if the mind, conscious of its own rectitude, is released from its earthly prison, and seeks heaven in free flight, doth it not despise all earthly things when it rejoices in its deliverance from earthly bonds, and enters upon the joys of heaven?'

SONG VII.

GLORY MAY NOT LAST.

Oh, let him, who pants for glory's guerdon,
Deeming glory all in all,
Look and see how wide the heaven expandeth,
Earth's enclosing bounds how small!

Shame it is, if your proud-swelling glory
May not fill this narrow room!
Why, then, strive so vainly, oh, ye proud ones!
To escape your mortal doom?

Though your name, to distant regions bruited,
O'er the earth be widely spread,
Though full many a lofty-sounding title
On your house its lustre shed,

Death at all this pomp and glory spurneth
When his hour draweth nigh,
Shrouds alike th' exalted and the humble,
Levels lowest and most high.

Where are now the bones of stanch
Fabricius?
Brutus, Cato—where are they?
Lingering fame, with a few graven letters,
Doth their empty name display.

But to know the great dead is not given
From a gilded name alone;
Nay, ye all alike must lie forgotten,
'Tis not *you* that fame makes known.

Fondly do ye deem life's little hour
Lengthened by fame's mortal breath;
There but waits you—when this, too, is
taken—
At the last a second death.

VIII.

'But that thou mayst not think that I wage implacable warfare against Fortune, I own there is a time when the deceitful goddess serves men well—I mean when she reveals herself, uncovers her face, and confesses her true character. Perhaps thou dost not yet grasp my meaning. Strange is the thing I am trying to express, and for this cause I can scarce find words to make clear my thought. For truly I believe that Ill Fortune is of more use to men than Good Fortune. For Good Fortune, when she wears the guise of happiness, and most seems to caress, is always lying; Ill Fortune is always truthful, since, in changing, she shows her inconstancy. The one deceives, the other teaches; the one enchains the minds of those who enjoy her favour by the semblance of delusive good, the other delivers them by the knowledge of the frail nature of happiness. Accordingly, thou mayst see the one fickle, shifting as the breeze, and ever self-deceived; the other sober-minded, alert, and wary, by reason of the very discipline of adversity. Finally, Good Fortune, by her allurements, draws men far from the true good; Ill Fortune ofttimes draws men back to true good with grappling-irons. Again, should it be esteemed a trifling boon, thinkest thou, that this cruel, this odious Fortune hath discovered to thee the hearts of thy faithful friends—that other hid from thee alike the faces of the true friends and of the false, but in departing she hath taken away *her* friends, and left thee *thine?* What price wouldst thou not have given for this service in the fulness of thy prosperity when thou seemedst to thyself fortunate? Cease, then, to seek the wealth thou hast lost, since in true friends thou hast found the most precious of all riches.'

SONG VIII.

LOVE IS LORD OF ALL.

Why are Nature's changes bound
To a fixed and ordered round?
What to leaguèd peace hath bent
Every warring element?

Wherefore doth the rosy morn
Rise on Phœbus' car upborne?
Why should Phœbe rule the night,
Led by Hesper's guiding light?
What the power that doth restrain
In his place the restless main,
That within fixed bounds he keeps,
Nor o'er earth in deluge sweeps?
Love it is that holds the chains,
Love o'er sea and earth that reigns;
Love—whom else but sovereign Love?—
Love, high lord in heaven above!
Yet should he his care remit,
All that now so close is knit
In sweet love and holy peace,
Would no more from conflict cease,
But with strife's rude shock and jar
All the world's fair fabric mar.
    Tribes and nations Love unites
By just treaty's sacred rites;
Wedlock's bonds he sanctifies
By affection's softest ties.
Love appointeth, as is due,
Faithful laws to comrades true—
Love, all-sovereign Love!—oh, then,
Ye are blest, ye sons of men,
If the love that rules the sky
In your hearts is throned on high!

BOOK III.

TRUE HAPPINESS AND FALSE.

SUMMARY.

CH. I. Boethius beseeches Philosophy to continue. She promises to lead him to true happiness.—CH. II. Happiness is the one end which all created beings seek. They aim variously at (*a*) wealth, or (*b*) rank, or (*c*) sovereignty, or (*d*) glory, or (*e*) pleasure, because they think thereby to attain either (*a*) contentment, (*b*) reverence, (*c*) power, (*d*) renown, or (*e*) gladness of heart, in one or other of which they severally imagine happiness to consist.—CH. III. Philosophy proceeds to consider whether happiness can really be secured in any of these ways. (*a*) So far from bringing contentment, riches only add to men's wants.—CH. IV. (*b*) High position cannot of itself win respect. Titles command no reverence in distant and bar-

barous lands. They even fall into contempt through lapse of time.—CH. V. (*c*) Sovereignty cannot even bestow safety. History tells of the downfall of kings and their ministers. Tyrants go in fear of their lives. —CH. VI. (*d*) Fame conferred on the unworthy is but disgrace. The splendour of noble birth is not a man's own, but his ancestors'.—CH. VII. (*e*) Pleasure begins in the restlessness of desire, and ends in repentance. Even the pure pleasures of home may turn to gall and bitterness.—CH. VIII. All fail, then, to give what they promise. There is, moreover, some accompanying evil involved in each of these aims. Beauty and bodily strength are likewise of little worth. In strength man is surpassed by the brutes; beauty is but outward show.—CH. IX. The source of men's error in following these phantoms of good is that *they break up and separate that which is in its nature one and indivisible.* Contentment, power, reverence, renown, and joy are essentially bound up one with the other, and, if they are to be attained at all, must be attained *together*. True happiness, if it can be found, will include them all. But it cannot be found among the perishable things hitherto considered.—CH. X. Such a happiness necessarily exists. Its seat is in God. Nay, God is very happiness, and in a manner, therefore, the happy man partakes also of the

Divine nature. All other ends are relative to this good, since they are all pursued only for the sake of good; it is *good* which is the sole ultimate end. And since the sole end is also happiness, it is plain that this good and happiness are in essence the same.—CH. XI. Unity is another aspect of goodness. Now, all things subsist so long only as they preserve the unity of their being; when they lose this unity, they perish. But the bent of nature forces all things (plants and inanimate things, as well as animals) to strive to continue in life. Therefore, all things desire unity, for unity is essential to life. But unity and goodness were shown to be the same. Therefore, good is proved to be the end towards which the whole universe tends.*—CH. XII. Boethius acknowledges that he is but recollecting truths he once knew. Philosophy goes on to show that it is goodness also by which the whole world is governed.† Boethius professes compunction for his former folly. But the paradox of evil is introduced, and he is once more perplexed.

---

* This solves the second of the points left in doubt at the end of bk. i., ch. vi.

† This solves the third. No distinct account is given of the first, but an answer may be gathered from the general argument of bks. ii., iii., and iv.

BOOK III.

I.

SHE ceased, but I stood fixed by the sweetness of the song in wonderment and eager expectation, my ears still strained to listen. And then after a little I said: 'Thou sovereign solace of the stricken soul, what refreshment hast thou brought me, no less by the sweetness of thy singing than by the weightiness of thy discourse! Verily, I think not that I shall hereafter be unequal to the blows of Fortune. Wherefore, I no longer dread the remedies which thou saidst were something too severe for my strength; nay, rather, I am eager to hear of them and call for them with all vehemence.'

Then said she: 'I marked thee fastening upon my words silently and intently, and I expected, or—to speak more truly—I myself brought about in thee, this state of mind. What now remains is of such sort that to the taste indeed it is biting, but when received within it turns to sweetness. But whereas thou dost profess thyself desirous of hearing, with what ardour wouldst thou not burn didst thou but perceive whither it is my task to lead thee!'

'Whither?' said I.

'To true felicity,' said she, 'which even now thy spirit sees in dreams, but cannot behold in very truth, while thine eyes are engrossed with semblances.'

Then said I: 'I beseech thee, do thou show to me her true shape without a moment's loss.'

'Gladly will I, for thy sake,' said she. 'But first I will try to sketch in words, and describe a cause which is more familiar to thee, that, when thou hast viewed this carefully, thou mayst turn thy eyes the other way, and recognise the beauty of true happiness.'

SONG I.

THE THORNS OF ERROR.

Who fain would sow the fallow field,
And see the growing corn,
Must first remove the useless weeds,
The bramble and the thorn.

After ill savour, honey's taste
Is to the mouth more sweet;
After the storm, the twinkling stars
The eyes more cheerly greet.

When night hath past, the bright dawn comes
In car of rosy hue;
So drive the false bliss from thy mind,
And thou shalt see the true.

II.

For a little space she remained in a fixed gaze, withdrawn, as it were, into the august chamber of her mind; then she thus began:

'All mortal creatures in those anxious aims which find employment in so many varied pursuits, though they take many paths, yet strive to reach one goal—the goal of happiness. Now, *the good* is that which, when a man hath got, he can lack nothing further. This it is which is the supreme good of all, containing within itself all particular good; so that if anything is still wanting thereto, this cannot be the supreme good, since something would be left outside which might be desired. 'Tis clear, then, that happiness is a state perfected by the assembling together of all good things. To this state, as we have said, all men try to attain, but by different paths. For the desire of the true good is naturally implanted in the minds of men; only error leads them aside out of the way in pursuit of the false. Some, deeming it the highest good to want for nothing, spare no pains to attain affluence; others, judging the good to be that to which respect is most worthily paid, strive to win the reverence of their fellow-citizens by the attainment of official dignity. Some there are who fix the chief good in supreme power; these either wish themselves to enjoy sovereignty, or try to attach themselves to those who have it. Those, again, who think renown to be something of supreme excellence are in haste to spread abroad the glory of their name either through the arts of war or of peace. A great many measure the attainment of good by joy and gladness of heart; these think it the height of happiness to give themselves over to pleasure. Others there are, again, who interchange the ends and means one with the other in their aims; for instance, some want riches for the sake of pleasure and power, some covet power either for the sake of money or in order to bring renown to their name. So it is on these ends, then, that the aim of human acts and wishes is centred, and on others like to these—for instance, noble birth and popularity, which seem to compass a certain renown; wife and children, which are sought for the sweetness of their possession; while as for friendship, the most sacred kind indeed is counted in the category of virtue, not of fortune; but other kinds are entered upon for the sake of power or of enjoyment. And as for bodily excellences, it is obvious that they are to be ranged with the above. For strength and stature surely manifest power; beauty and fleetness of foot bring celebrity; health brings pleasure. It is plain, then, that the only object sought for in all these ways is *happiness*. For that which each seeks in preference to all else, that is in his judgment the supreme good. And we have defined the supreme good to be happiness. Therefore, that state which each wishes in preference to all others is in his judgment happy.

'Thou hast, then, set before thine eyes something like a scheme of human happiness—wealth, rank, power, glory, pleasure.

Now Epicurus, from a sole regard to these considerations, with some consistency concluded the highest good to be pleasure, because all the other objects seem to bring some delight to the soul. But to return to human pursuits and aims: man's mind seeks to recover its proper good, in spite of the mistiness of its recollection, but, like a drunken man, knows not by what path to return home. Think you they are wrong who strive to escape want? Nay, truly there is nothing which can so well complete happiness as a state abounding in all good things, needing nothing from outside, but wholly self-sufficing. Do they fall into error who deem that which is best to be also best deserving to receive the homage of reverence? Not at all. That cannot possibly be vile and contemptible, to attain which the endeavours of nearly all mankind are directed. Then, is power not to be reckoned in the category of good? Why, can that which is plainly more efficacious than anything else be esteemed a thing feeble and void of strength? Or is renown to be thought of no account? Nay, it cannot be ignored that the highest renown is constantly associated with the highest excellence. And what need is there to say that happiness is not haunted by care and gloom, nor exposed to trouble and vexation, since that is a condition we ask of the very least of things, from the possession and enjoyment of which we expect delight? So, then, these are the blessings men wish to win; they want riches, rank, sovereignty, glory, pleasure, because they believe that by these means they will secure independence, reverence, power, renown, and joy of heart. Therefore, it is *the good* which men seek by such divers courses; and herein is easily shown the might of Nature's power, since, although opinions are so various and discordant, yet they agree in cherishing *good* as the end.'

SONG II.

The Bent of Nature.

How the might of Nature sways
All the world in ordered ways,
How resistless laws control
Each least portion of the whole—
Fain would I in sounding verse
On my pliant strings rehearse.
Lo, the lion captive ta'en
Meekly wears his gilded chain ;
Yet though he by hand be fed,
Though a master's whip he dread,
If but once the taste of gore
Whet his cruel lips once more,
Straight his slumbering fierceness wakes,
With one roar his bonds he breaks,
And first wreaks his vengeful force
On his trainer's mangled corse.
And the woodland songster, pent
In forlorn imprisonment,
Though a mistress' lavish care
Store of honeyed sweets prepare ;
Yet, if in his narrow cage,
As he hops from bar to bar,
He should spy the woods afar,

Cool with sheltering foliage,
All these dainties he will spurn,
To the woods his heart will turn ;
Only for the woods he longs,
Pipes the woods in all his songs.
  To rude force the sapling bends,
While the hand its pressure lends ;
If the hand its pressure slack,
Straight the supple wood springs back.
Phœbus in the western main
Sinks ; but swift his car again
By a secret path is borne
To the wonted gates of morn.
  Thus are all things seen to yearn
In due time for due return ;
And no order fixed may stay,
Save which in th' appointed way
Joins the end to the beginning
In a steady cycle spinning.

III.

'Ye, too, creatures of earth, have some glimmering of your origin, however faint, and though in a vision dim and clouded. yet in some wise, notwithstanding, ye discern the true end of happiness, and so the aim of nature leads you thither—to that true good—while error in many forms leads you astray therefrom. For reflect whether men are able to win happiness by those means through which they think to reach the proposed end. Truly, if either wealth, rank, or any of the rest, bring with them anything of such sort as seems to have nothing wanting to it that is good, we, too, acknowledge that some are made happy by the acquisition of these things. But if they are not able to fulfil their promises, and, moreover, lack many good things, is not the happiness men seek in them clearly discovered to be a false show?

Therefore do I first ask thee thyself, who but lately wert living in affluence, amid all that abundance of wealth, was thy mind never troubled in consequence of some wrong done to thee?'

'Nay,' said I, 'I cannot ever remember a time when my mind was so completely at peace as not to feel the pang of some uneasiness.'

'Was it not because either something was absent which thou wouldst not have absent, or present which thou wouldst have away?'

'Yes,' said I.

'Then, thou didst want the presence of the one, the absence of the other?'

'Admitted.'

'But a man lacks that of which he is in want?'

'He does.'

'And he who lacks something is not in all points self-sufficing?'

'No; certainly not,' said I.

'So wert thou, then, in the plenitude of thy wealth, supporting this insufficiency?'

'I must have been.'

'Wealth, then, cannot make its possessor independent and free from all want, yet this was what it seemed to promise. Moreover, I think this also well deserves to be considered—that there is nothing in the special nature of money to hinder its being taken away from those who possess it against their will.'

'I admit it.'

'Why, of course, when every day the stronger wrests it from the weaker without his consent. Else, whence come lawsuits, except in seeking to recover moneys which have been taken away against their owner's will by force or fraud?'

'True,' said I.

'Then, everyone will need some extraneous means of protection to keep his money safe.'

'Who can venture to deny it?'

'Yet he would not, unless he possessed the money which it is possible to lose.'

'No; he certainly would not.'

'Then, we have worked round to an opposite conclusion: the wealth which was thought to make a man independent rather puts him in need of further protection. How in the world, then, can want be driven away by riches? Cannot the rich feel hunger? Cannot they thirst? Are not the limbs of the wealthy sensitive to the winter's cold? "But," thou wilt say, "the rich have the wherewithal to sate their hunger, the means to get rid of thirst and cold." True enough; want can thus be soothed by riches, wholly removed it cannot be. For if this ever-gaping, ever-craving want is glutted by wealth, it needs must be that the want itself which can be so glutted still remains. I do not speak of how very little suffices for nature, and how for avarice nothing is enough. Wherefore, if wealth cannot get rid of want, and makes new wants of its own, how can ye believe that it bestows independence?'

SONG III.

THE INSATIABLENESS OF AVARICE.

Though the covetous grown wealthy
  See his piles of gold rise high;
Though he gather store of treasure
  That can never satisfy;
Though with pearls his gorget blazes,
  Rarest that the ocean yields;
Though a hundred head of oxen
  Travail in his ample fields;
Ne'er shall carking care forsake him
  While he draws this vital breath,
And his riches go not with him,
  When his eyes are closed in death.

IV.

'Well, but official dignity clothes him to whom it comes with honour and reverence! Have, then, offices of state such power as to plant virtue in the minds of their possessors, and drive out vice? Nay, they are rather wont to signalize iniquity than to chase it away, and hence arises our indignation that honours so often fall to the most iniquitous of men. Accordingly, Catullus calls Nonius an "ulcer-spot," though "sitting in the curule chair." Dost not see what infamy high position brings upon the bad? Surely their unworthiness will be less conspicuous if their rank does not draw upon them the public notice! In thy own case, wouldst thou ever have been induced by all these perils to think of sharing office with Decoratus, since thou hast discerned in him the spirit of a rascally parasite and informer? No; we cannot deem men worthy of reverence on account of their office, whom we deem unworthy of the office itself. But didst thou see a man endued with wisdom, couldst thou suppose him not worthy of reverence, nor of that wisdom with which he was endued?'

'No; certainly not.'

'There is in Virtue a dignity of her own which she forthwith passes over to those to whom she is united. And since public honours cannot do this, it is clear that they do not possess the true beauty of dignity. And here this well deserves to be noticed—that if a man is the more scorned in proportion as he is despised by a greater number, high position not only fails to win reverence for the wicked, but even loads them the more with contempt by drawing more attention to them. But not without retribution; for the wicked pay back a return in kind to the dignities they put on by the pollution of their touch. Perhaps, too, another consideration may teach thee to confess that true reverence cannot come through these counterfeit dignities. It is this: If one who had been many times consul chanced to visit barbaric lands, would his office win him the reverence of the barbarians? And yet if reverence were the natural effect of dignities, they would not forego their proper function in any part of the world, even as fire never anywhere fails to give forth heat. But since this effect is not due to their own efficacy, but is attached to them by the mistaken opinion of mankind, they disappear straightway when they are set before those who do not esteem them dignities. Thus the case stands with foreign peoples. But does their repute last for ever, even in the land of their origin? Why, the prefecture, which was once a great power, is now an empty name—a burden merely on the senator's fortune; the commissioner of the public corn supply was once a personage—now what is more contemptible than this office? For, as we said just now, that which hath no true comeliness of its own now receives, now loses, lustre at the caprice of those who have to do with it. So, then, if dignities cannot win men reverence, if they are actually sullied by the contamination of the wicked, if they lose their splendour through time's changes, if they come into contempt merely for lack of public estimation, what precious beauty have they in themselves, much less to give to others?'

SONG IV.

Disgrace of Honours conferred by a Tyrant.

Though royal purple soothes his pride,
  And snowy pearls his neck adorn,
Nero in all his riot lives
  The mark of universal scorn.

Yet he on reverend heads conferred
  Th' inglorious honours of the state.
Shall we, then, deem them truly blessed
  Whom such preferment hath made great?

V.

'Well, then, does sovereignty and the intimacy of kings prove able to confer power? Why, surely does not the happiness of kings endure for ever? And yet antiquity is full of examples, and these days also, of kings whose happiness has turned into calamity. How glorious a power, which is not even found effectual for its own preservation! But if happiness has its source in sovereign power, is not happiness diminished, and misery inflicted in its stead, in so far as that power falls short of completeness? Yet, however widely human sovereignty be extended, there must still be more peoples left, over whom each several king holds no sway. Now, at whatever point the power on which happiness depends ceases, here powerlessness steals in and makes wretchedness; so, by this way of reckoning, there must needs be a balance of wretchedness in the lot of the king. The tyrant who had made trial of the perils of his condition figured the fears that haunt a throne under the image of a sword hanging over a man's head.* What sort of power, then, is this which cannot drive away the gnawings of anxiety, or shun the stings of terror? Fain would they themselves have lived secure, but they cannot; then they boast about their power! Dost thou count him to possess power whom thou seest to wish what he cannot bring to pass? Dost thou count him to possess power who encompasses himself with a body-guard, who fears those he terrifies more than they fear him, who, to keep up the semblance of power, is himself at the mercy of his slaves? Need I say anything of the friends of kings, when I show royal dominion itself so utterly and miserably weak—why ofttimes the royal power in its plenitude brings them low, ofttimes involves them in its fall? Nero drove his friend and preceptor, Seneca, to the choice of the manner of his death. Antoninus exposed Papinianus, who was long power-

* The sword of Damocles.

ful at court, to the swords of the soldiery. Yet each of these was willing to renounce his power. Seneca tried to surrender his wealth also to Nero, and go into retirement; but neither achieved his purpose. When they tottered, their very greatness dragged them down. What manner of thing, then, is this power which keeps men in fear while they possess it—which when thou art fain to keep, thou art not safe, and when thou desirest to lay it aside, thou canst not rid thyself of? Are friends any protection who have been attached by fortune, not by virtue? Nay; him whom good fortune has made a friend, ill fortune will make an enemy. And what plague is more effectual to do hurt than a foe of one's own household?'

SONG V.

SELF-MASTERY.

Who on power sets his aim,
First must his own spirit tame;
He must shun his neck to thrust
'Neath th' unholy yoke of lust.
For, though India's far-off land
Bow before his wide command,
Utmost Thule homage pay—
If he cannot drive away
Haunting care and black distress,
In his power, he's powerless.

VI.

'Again, how misleading, how base, a thing ofttimes is glory! Well does the tragic poet exclaim:

"'Oh, fond Repute, how many a time and oft
Hast thou raised high in pride the base-born churl!'"

For many have won a great name through the mistaken beliefs of the multitude—and what can be imagined more shameful than that? Nay, they who are praised falsely must needs themselves blush at their own praises! And even when praise is won by merit, still, how does it add to the good conscience of the wise man who measures his good not by popular repute, but by the truth of inner conviction? And if at all it does seem a fair thing to get this same renown spread abroad, it follows that any failure so to spread it is held foul. But if, as I set forth but now, there must needs be many tribes and peoples whom the fame of any single man cannot reach, it follows that he whom thou esteemest glorious seems all inglorious in a neighbouring quarter of the globe. As to popular favour, I do not think it even worthy of mention in this place, since it never cometh of judgment, and never lasteth steadily.

'Then, again, who does not see how empty, how foolish, is the fame of noble birth? Why, if the nobility is based on renown, the renown is another's! For, truly, nobility seems to be a sort of reputation coming from the merits of ancestors. But if it is the praise which brings renown, of necessity it is they who are praised that are famous. Wherefore, the fame of another clothes thee not with splendour if thou hast none of thine own. So, if there is any excellence in nobility of birth, methinks it is this alone—that it would seem to impose upon the nobly born the obligation not to degenerate from the virtue of their ancestors.'

SONG VI.

TRUE NOBILITY.

All men are of one kindred stock, though
  scattered far and wide;
For one is Father of us all—one doth for
  all provide.
He gave the sun his golden beams, the
  moon her silver horn;
He set mankind upon the earth, as stars
  the heavens adorn.
He shut a soul—a heaven-born soul—
  within the body's frame;
The noble origin he gave each mortal
  wight may claim.
Why boast ye, then, so loud of race and
  high ancestral line?
If ye behold your being's source, and
  God's supreme design,
None is degenerate, none base, unless by
  taint of sin
And cherished vice he foully stain his
  heavenly origin.

VII.

'Then, what shall I say of the pleasures of the body? The lust thereof is full of uneasiness; the sating, of repentance. What sicknesses, what intolerable pains, are they wont to bring on the bodies of those who enjoy them—the fruits of iniquity, as it were! Now, what sweetness the stimulus of pleasure may have I do not know. But that the issues of pleasure are painful everyone may understand who chooses to recall the memory of his own fleshly lusts. Nay, if these can make happiness, there is no reason why the beasts also should not be happy, since all their efforts are eagerly set upon satisfying the bodily wants. I know, indeed, that the sweetness of wife and children should be right comely, yet only too true to nature is what was said of one—that he found in his sons his tormentors. And how galling such a contingency would be, I must needs put thee in mind, since thou hast never in any wise suffered such experiences, nor art thou now under any uneasiness. In such a case, I agree with my servant Euripides, who said that a man without children was fortunate in his misfortune.'*

SONG VII.

PLEASURE'S STING.

This is the way of Pleasure :
She stings them that despoil her ;
And, like the wingèd toiler
Who's lost her honeyed treasure,
She flies, but leaves her smart
Deep-rankling in the heart.

* Paley translates the lines in Euripides' 'Andromache': 'They [the childless] are indeed spared from much pain and sorrow, but their supposed happiness is after all but wretchedness.' Euripides' meaning is therefore really just the reverse of that which Boethius makes it. See Euripides, 'Andromache,' ll. 418-420.

VIII.

'It is beyond doubt, then, that these paths do not lead to happiness; they cannot guide anyone to the promised goal. Now, I will very briefly show what serious evils are involved in following them. Just consider. Is it thy endeavour to heap up money? Why, thou must wrest it from its present possessor! Art thou minded to put on the splendour of official dignity? Thou must beg from those who have the giving of it; thou who covetest to outvie others in honour must lower thyself to the humble posture of petition. Dost thou long for power? Thou must face perils, for thou wilt be at the mercy of thy subjects' plots. Is glory thy aim? Thou art lured on through all manner of hardships, and there is an end to thy peace of mind. Art fain to lead a life of pleasure? Yet who does not scorn and contemn one who is the slave of the weakest and vilest of things—the body? Again, on how slight and perishable a possession do they rely who set before themselves bodily excellences! Can ye ever surpass the elephant in bulk or the bull in strength? Can ye excel the tiger in swiftness? Look upon the infinitude, the solidity, the swift motion, of the heavens, and for once cease to admire things mean and worthless. And yet the heavens are not so much to be admired on this account as for the reason which guides them. Then, how transient is the lustre of beauty! how soon gone!—more fleeting than the fading bloom of spring flowers. And yet if, as Aristotle says, men should see with the eyes of Lynceus, so that their sight might pierce through obstructions, would not that body of Alcibiades, so gloriously fair in outward seeming, appear altogether loathsome when all its inward parts lay open to the view? Therefore, it is not thy own nature that makes thee seem beautiful, but the weakness of the eyes that see thee. Yet prize as unduly as ye will that body's excellences; so long as ye know that this that ye admire, whatever its worth, can be dissolved away by the feeble flame of a three days' fever. From all which considerations we may conclude as a whole, that these things which cannot make good the advantages they promise, which are never made perfect by the assemblage of all good things—these neither lead as by-ways to happiness, nor themselves make men completely happy.'

SONG VIII.

HUMAN FOLLY.

Alas! how wide astray
Doth Ignorance these wretched mortals lead
From Truth's own way!
For not on leafy stems
Do ye within the green wood look for gold,
Nor strip the vine for gems;

Your nets ye do not spread
Upon the hill-tops, that the groaning board
With fish be furnishèd;
If ye are fain to chase
The bounding goat, ye sweep not in vain search
The ocean's ruffled face.

The sea's far depths they know,
Each hidden nook, wherein the waves o'erwash
The pearl as white as snow ;
Where lurks the Tyrian shell,
Where fish and prickly urchins do abound,
All this they know full well.

But not to know or care
Where hidden lies the good all hearts desire—
This blindness they can bear ;
With gaze on earth low-bent,
They seek for that which reacheth far beyond
The starry firmament.

What curse shall I call down
On hearts so dull ? May they the race still run
For wealth and high renown !
And when with much ado
The false good they have grasped—ah, then too late !—
May they discern the true !

IX.

'This much may well suffice to set forth the form of false happiness; if this is now clear to thine eyes, the next step is to show what true happiness is.'

'Indeed,' said I, 'I see clearly enough that neither is independence to be found in wealth, nor power in sovereignty, nor reverence in dignities, nor fame in glory, nor true joy in pleasures.'

'Hast thou discerned also the causes why this is so?'

'I seem to have some inkling, but I should like to learn more at large from thee.'

'Why, truly the reason is hard at hand. *That which is simple and indivisible by nature human error separates*, and transforms from the true and perfect to the false and imperfect. Dost thou imagine that which lacketh nothing can want power?'

'Certainly not.'

'Right; for if there is any feebleness of strength in anything, in this there must necessarily be need of external protection.'

'That is so.'

'Accordingly, the nature of independence and power is one and the same.'

'It seems so.'

'Well, but dost think that anything of such a nature as this can be looked upon with contempt, or is it rather of all things most worthy of veneration?'

'Nay; there can be no doubt as to that.'

'Let us, then, add reverence to independence and power, and conclude these three to be one.'

'We must if we will acknowledge the truth.'

'Thinkest thou, then, this combination of qualities to be obscure and without distinction, or rather famous in all renown? Just consider: can that want renown which has been agreed to be lacking in nothing, to be supreme in power, and right worthy of honour, for the reason that it cannot bestow this upon itself, and so comes to appear somewhat poor in esteem?'

'I cannot but acknowledge that, being what it is, this union of qualities is also right famous.'

'It follows, then, that we must admit that renown is not different from the other three.'

'It does,' said I.

'That, then, which needs nothing outside itself, which can accomplish all things in its own strength, which enjoys fame and compels reverence, must not this evidently be also fully crowned with joy?'

'In sooth, I cannot conceive,' said I, 'how any sadness can find entrance into such a state; wherefore I must needs acknowledge it full of joy—at least, if our former conclusions are to hold.'

'Then, for the same reasons, this also is necessary—that independence, power, renown, reverence, and sweetness of delight, are different only in name, but in substance differ no wise one from the other.'

'It is,' said I.

'This, then, which is one, and simple by nature, human perversity separates, and, in trying to win a part of that which has no parts, fails to attain not only that portion (since there are no portions), but also the whole, to which it does not dream of aspiring.'

'How so?' said I.

'He who, to escape want, seeks riches, gives himself no concern about power; he prefers a mean and low estate, and also denies himself many pleasures dear to nature to avoid losing the money which he has gained. But at this rate he does not even attain to independence—a weakling void of strength, vexed by distresses, mean and despised, and buried in obscurity. He, again, who thirsts alone for power squanders his wealth, despises pleasure, and thinks fame and rank alike worthless without power. But thou seest in how many ways his state also is defective. Sometimes it happens that he lacks necessaries, that he is gnawed by anxieties, and, since he cannot rid himself of these inconveniences, even ceases to have that power which was his whole end and aim. In like manner may we cast up the reckoning in case of rank, of glory, or of pleasure. For since each one of these severally is identical with the rest, whosoever seeks any one of them without the others does not even lay hold of that one which he makes his aim.'

'Well,' said I, 'what then?'

'Suppose anyone desire to obtain them together, he does indeed wish for happiness as a whole; but will he find it in these things which, as we have proved, are unable to bestow what they promise?'

'Nay; by no means,' said I.

'Then, happiness must certainly not be sought in these things which severally are believed to afford some one of the blessings most to be desired.'

'They must not, I admit. No conclusion could be more true.'

'So, then, the form and the causes of false happiness are set before thine eyes. Now turn thy gaze to the other side; there thou wilt straightway see the true happiness I promised.'

'Yea, indeed, 'tis plain to the blind,' said I. 'Thou didst point it out even now in seeking to unfold the causes of the false. For, unless I am mistaken, that is true and perfect happiness which crowns one with the union of independence, power, reverence, renown, and joy. And to prove to thee with how deep an insight I have listened—since all these are the same—that which can truly bestow one of them I know to be without doubt full and complete happiness.'

'Happy art thou, my scholar, in this thy conviction; only one thing shouldst thou add.'

'What is that?' said I.

'Is there aught, thinkest thou, amid these mortal and perishable things which can produce a state such as this?'

'Nay, surely not; and this thou hast so amply demonstrated that no word more is needed.'

'Well, then, these things seem to give to mortals shadows of the true good, or some kind of imperfect good; but the true and perfect good they cannot bestow.'

'Even so,' said I.

'Since, then, thou hast learnt what that true happiness is, and what men falsely call happiness, it now remains that thou shouldst learn from what source to seek this.'

'Yes; to this I have long been eagerly looking forward.'

'Well, since, as Plato maintains in the "Timæus," we ought even in the most trivial matters to implore the Divine protection, what thinkest thou should we now do in order to deserve to find the seat of that highest good?'

'We must invoke the Father of all things,' said I; 'for without this no enterprise sets out from a right beginning.'

'Thou sayest well,' said she; and forthwith lifted up her voice and sang:

SONG IX.*

INVOCATION.

Maker of earth and sky, from age to age
Who rul'st the world by reason; at whose word
Time issues from Eternity's abyss:
To all that moves the source of movement, fixed
Thyself and moveless. Thee no cause impelled
Extrinsic this proportioned frame to shape
From shapeless matter; but, deep-set within
Thy inmost being, the form of perfect good,
From envy free; and Thou didst mould the whole
To that supernal pattern. Beauteous
The world in Thee thus imaged, being Thyself

* The substance of this poem is taken from Plato's 'Timæus,' 29-42. See Jowett, vol. iii., pp. 448-462 (third edition).

Most beautiful. So Thou the work didst fashion
In that fair likeness, bidding it put on
Perfection through the exquisite perfectness
Of every part's contrivance.
Thou dost bind
The elements in balanced harmony,
So that the hot and cold, the moist and dry,
Contend not; nor the pure fire leaping up
Escape, or weight of waters whelm the earth.
Thou joinest and diffusest through the whole,
Linking accordantly its several parts,
A soul of threefold nature, moving all.
This, cleft in twain, and in two circles gathered,
Speeds in a path that on itself returns,
Encompassing mind's limits, and conforms
The heavens to her true semblance. Lesser souls
And lesser lives by a like ordinance
Thou sendest forth, each to its starry car
Affixing, and dost strew them far and wide

9—2

O'er earth and heaven. These by a law benign
Thou biddest turn again, and render back
To thee their fires.
Oh, grant, almighty Father,
Grant us on reason's wing to soar aloft
To heaven's exalted height; grant us to see
The fount of good; grant us, the true light found,
To fix our steadfast eyes in vision clear
On Thee. Disperse the heavy mists of earth,
And shine in Thine own splendour. For Thou art
The true serenity and perfect rest
Of every pious soul—to see Thy face,
The end and the beginning—One the guide,
The traveller, the pathway, and the goal.

X.

'Since now thou hast seen what is the form of the imperfect good, and what the form of the perfect also, methinks I should next show in what manner this perfection of felicity is built up. And here I conceive it proper to inquire, first, whether any excellence, such as thou hast lately defined, can exist in the nature of things, lest we be deceived by an empty fiction of thought to which no true reality answers. But it cannot be denied that such does exist, and is, as it were, the source of all things good. For everything which is called imperfect is spoken of as imperfect by reason of the privation of some perfection; so it comes to pass that, whenever imperfection is found in any particular, there must necessarily be a perfection in respect of that particular also. For were there no such perfection, it is utterly inconceivable how that so-called *im*perfection should come into existence. Nature does not make a beginning with things mutilated and imperfect; she starts with what is whole and perfect, and falls away later to these feeble and inferior productions. So if there is, as we showed before, a happiness of a frail and imperfect kind, it cannot be doubted but there is also a happiness substantial and perfect.'

'Most true is thy conclusion, and most sure,' said I.

'Next to consider where the dwelling-place of this happiness may be. The common belief of all mankind agrees that God, the supreme of all things, is good. For since nothing can be imagined better than God, how can we doubt Him to be good than whom there is nothing better? Now, reason shows God to be good in such wise as to prove that in Him is perfect good. For were it not so, He would not be supreme of all things; for there would be something else more excellent, possessed of perfect good, which would seem to have the advantage in priority and dignity, since it has clearly appeared that all perfect things are prior to those less complete. Wherefore, lest we fall into an infinite regression, we must acknowledge the supreme God to be full of supreme and perfect good. But we have determined that true happiness is the perfect good; therefore true happiness must dwell in the supreme Deity.'

'I accept thy reasonings,' said I; 'they cannot in any wise be disputed.'

'But, come, see how strictly and incontrovertibly thou mayst prove this our assertion that the supreme Godhead hath fullest possession of the highest good.'

'In what way, pray?' said I.

'Do not rashly suppose that He who is the Father of all things hath received that highest good of which He is said to be possessed either from some external source, or hath it as a natural endowment in such sort that thou mightest consider the essence of the happiness possessed, and of the God who possesses it, distinct and different. For if thou deemest it received from without, thou mayst esteem that which gives more excellent than that which has received. But Him we most worthily acknowledge to be the most supremely excellent of all things. If, however, it is in Him by nature, yet is logically distinct, the thought is inconceivable, since we are speaking of God, who is supreme of all things. Who was there to join these distinct essences? Finally, when one thing is different from another, the things so conceived as distinct cannot be identical. Therefore that which of its own nature is distinct from the highest good is not itself the highest good—an impious thought of Him than whom, 'tis plain, nothing can be more excellent. For universally nothing can be better in nature than the source from which it has come; therefore on most true grounds of reason would I conclude that which is the source of all things to be in its own essence the highest good.'

'And most justly,' said I.

'But the highest good has been admitted to be happiness.'

'Yes.'

'Then,' said she, 'it is necessary to acknowledge that God is very happiness.'

'Yes,' said I; 'I cannot gainsay my former admissions, and I see clearly that this is a necessary inference therefrom.'

'Reflect, also,' said she, 'whether the same conclusion is not further confirmed by considering that there cannot be two supreme goods distinct one from the other. For the goods which are different clearly cannot be severally each what the other is: wherefore neither of the two can be perfect, since to either the other is wanting; but since it is not perfect, it cannot manifestly be the supreme good. By no means, then, can goods which are supreme be different one from the other. But we have concluded that both happiness and God are the supreme good; wherefore that which is highest Divinity must also itself necessarily be supreme happiness.'

'No conclusion,' said I, 'could be truer to fact, nor more soundly reasoned out, nor more worthy of God.'

'Then, further,' said she, 'just as geometricians are wont to draw inferences from their demonstrations to which they give the name "deductions," so will I add here a sort of corollary. For since men become happy by the acquisition of happiness, while happiness is very Godship, it is manifest that they become happy by the acquisition of Godship. But as by the acquisition of justice men become just, and wise by the acquisition of wisdom, so by parity of reasoning by acquiring Godship they must of necessity become gods. So every man who is happy is a god; and though in nature God is One only, yet there is nothing to hinder that very many should be gods by participation in that nature.'

'A fair conclusion, and a precious,' said I, 'deduction or corollary, by whichever name thou wilt call it.'

'And yet,' said she, 'not one whit fairer than this which reason persuades us to add.'

'Why, what?' said I.

'Why, seeing happiness has many particulars included under it, should all these be regarded as forming one body of happiness, as it were, made up of various parts, or is there some one of them which forms the full essence of happiness, while all the rest are relative to this?'

'I would thou wouldst unfold the whole matter to me at large.'

'We judge happiness to be good, do we not?'

'Yea, the supreme good.'

'And this superlative applies to all; for this same happiness is adjudged to be the completest independence, the highest power, reverence, renown, and pleasure.'

'What then?'

'Are all these goods—independence, power, and the rest—to be deemed members of happiness, as it were, or are they all relative to good as to their summit and crown?'

'I understand the problem, but I desire to hear how thou wouldst solve it.'

'Well, then, listen to the determination of the matter. Were all these members composing happiness, they would differ severally one from the other. For this is the nature of parts—that by their difference they compose one body. All these, however, have been proved to be the same; therefore they cannot possibly be members, otherwise happiness will seem to be built up out of one member, which cannot be.'

'There can be no doubt as to that,' said I; 'but I am impatient to hear what remains.'

'Why, it is manifest that all the others

are relative to the good. For the very reason why independence is sought is that it is judged good, and so power also, because it is believed to be good. The same, too, may be supposed of reverence, of renown, and of pleasant delight. Good, then, is the sum and source of all desirable things. That which has not in itself any good, either in reality or in semblance, can in no wise be desired. Contrariwise, even things which by nature are not good are desired as if they were truly good, if they seem to be so. Whereby it comes to pass that goodness is rightly believed to be the sum and hinge and cause of all things desirable. Now, that for the sake of which anything is desired itself seems to be most wished for. For instance, if anyone wishes to ride for the sake of health, he does not so much wish for the exercise of riding as the benefit of his health. Since, then, all things are sought for the sake of the good, it is not these so much as good itself that is sought by all. But that on account of which all other things are wished for was, we agreed, happiness; wherefore thus also it appears that it is happiness alone which is sought. From all which it is transparently clear that the essence of absolute good and of happiness is one and the same.'

'I cannot see how anyone can dissent from these conclusions.'

'But we have also proved that God and true happiness are one and the same.'

'Yes,' said I.

'Then we can safely conclude, also, that God's essence is seated in absolute good, and nowhere else.'

SONG X.

THE TRUE LIGHT.

Hither come, all ye whose minds
Lust with rosy fetters binds—
Lust to bondage hard compelling
Th' earthy souls that are his dwelling—
Here shall be your labour's close;
Here your haven of repose.
Come, to your one refuge press;
Wide it stands to all distress!
Not the glint of yellow gold
Down bright Hermus' current rolled;

Not the Tagus' precious sands,
Nor in far-off scorching lands
All the radiant gems that hide
Under Indus' storied tide—
Emerald green and glistering white—
Can illume our feeble sight;
But they rather leave the mind
In its native darkness blind.
For the fairest beams they shed
In earth's lowest depths were fed;
But the splendour that supplies
Strength and vigour to the skies,
And the universe controls,
Shunneth dark and ruined souls.
He who once hath seen *this* light
Will not call the sunbeam bright.

XI.

'I quite agree,' said I, 'truly all thy reasonings hold admirably together.'

Then said she: 'What value wouldst thou put upon the boon shouldst thou come to the knowledge of the absolute good?'

'Oh, an infinite,' said I, 'if only I were so blest as to learn to know God also who is the good.'

'Yet this will I make clear to thee on truest grounds of reason, if only our recent conclusions stand fast.'

'They will.'

'Have we not shown that those things which most men desire are not true and perfect good precisely for this cause—that they differ severally one from another, and, seeing that one is wanting to another, they cannot bestow full and absolute good; but that they become the true good when they are gathered, as it were, into one form and agency, so that that which is independence is likewise power, reverence, renown, and pleasant delight, and unless they are all one and the same, they have no claim to be counted among things desirable?'

'Yes; this was clearly proved, and cannot in any wise be doubted.'

'Now, when things are far from being good while they are different, but become good as soon as they are one, is it not true that these become good by acquiring unity?'

'It seems so,' said I.

'But dost not thou allow that all which is good is good by participation in goodness?'

'It is.'

'Then, thou must on similar grounds admit that unity and goodness are the same; for when the effects of things in their natural working differ not, their essence is one and the same.'

'There is no denying it.'

'Now, dost thou know,' said she, 'that all which is abides and subsists so long as it continues one, but so soon as it ceases to be one it perishes and falls to pieces?'

'In what way?'

'Why, take animals, for example. When soul and body come together, and continue in one, this is, we say, a living creature; but when this unity is broken by the separation of these two, the creature dies, and is clearly no longer living. The body also, while it remains in one form by the joining together of its members, presents a human appearance; but if the separation and dispersal of the parts break up the body's unity, it ceases to be what it was. And if we extend our survey to all other things, without doubt it will manifestly appear that each several thing subsists while it is one, but when it ceases to be one perishes.'

'Yes; when I consider further, I see it to be even as thou sayest.'

'Well, is there aught,' said she, 'which, in so far as it acts conformably to nature, abandons the wish for life, and desires to come to death and corruption?'

'Looking to living creatures, which have some faults of choice, I find none that, without external compulsion, forego the will to live, and of their own accord hasten

10

to destruction. For every creature diligently pursues the end of self-preservation, and shuns death and destruction. As to herbs and trees, and inanimate things generally, I am altogether in doubt what to think.'

'And yet there is no possibility of question about this either, since thou seest how herbs and trees grow in places suitable for them, where, as far as their nature admits, they cannot quickly wither and die. Some spring up in the plains, others in the mountains; some grow in marshes, others cling to rocks; and others, again, find a fertile soil in the barren sands; and if you try to transplant these elsewhere, they wither away. Nature gives to each the soil that suits it, and uses her diligence to prevent any of them dying, so long as it is possible for them to continue alive. Why do they all draw their nourishment from roots as from a mouth dipped into the earth, and distribute the strong bark over the pith? Why are all the softer parts like the pith deeply encased within, while the external parts have the strong texture of wood, and outside of all is the bark to resist the weather's inclemency, like a champion stout in endurance? Again, how great is nature's diligence to secure universal propagation by multiplying seed! Who does not know all these to be contrivances, not only for the present maintenance of a species, but for its lasting continuance, generation after generation, for ever? And do not also the things believed inanimate on like grounds of reason seek each what is proper to itself? Why do the flames shoot lightly upward, while the earth presses downward with its weight, if it is not that these motions and situations are suitable to their respective natures? Moreover, each several thing is preserved by that which is agreeable to its nature, even as it is destroyed by things inimical. Things solid like stones resist disintegration by the close adhesion of their parts. Things fluid like air and water yield easily to what divides them, but swiftly flow back and mingle with those parts from which they have been severed, while fire, again, refuses to be cut at all. And we are not now treating of the voluntary motions of an intelligent soul, but of the drift of nature. Even so is it that we digest our food without thinking about it, and draw our breath unconsciously in sleep; nay, even in living creatures the love of life cometh not of conscious will, but from the principles of nature. For oftentimes in the stress of circumstances will chooses the death which nature shrinks from; and contrarily, in spite of natural appetite, will restrains that work of reproduction by which alone the persistence of perishable creatures is maintained. So entirely does this love of self come from drift of nature, not from animal impulse. Providence has furnished things with this most cogent reason for continuance: they must desire life, so long as it is naturally possible for them to continue living. Wherefore in no way mayst thou doubt but that things naturally aim at continuance of existence, and shun destruction.'

'I confess,' said I, 'that what I lately thought uncertain, I now perceive to be indubitably clear.'

'Now, that which seeks to subsist and continue desires to be one; for if its oneness be gone, its very existence cannot continue.'

'True,' said I.

'All things, then, desire to be one.'

'I agree.'

'But we have proved that one is the very same thing as good.'

'We have.'

'All things, then, seek the good; indeed, you may express the fact by defining good as that which all desire.'

'Nothing could be more truly thought out. Either there is no single end to which all things are relative, or else the end to which all things universally hasten must be the highest good of all.'

Then she: 'Exceedingly do I rejoice, dear pupil; thine eye is now fixed on the very central mark of truth. Moreover, herein is revealed that of which thou didst erstwhile profess thyself ignorant.'

'What is that?' said I.

'The end and aim of the whole universe. Surely it is that which is desired of all; and, since we have concluded the good to be such, we ought to acknowledge the end and aim of the whole universe to be "the good."'

SONG XI.

Reminiscence.*

Who truth pursues, who from false ways
  His heedful steps would keep,
By inward light must search within
  In meditation deep;
All outward bent he must repress
His soul's true treasure to possess.

Then all that error's mists obscured
  Shall shine more clear than light,
This fleshly frame's oblivious weight
  Hath quenched not reason quite;
The germs of truth still lie within,
Whence we by learning all may win.

Else how could ye the answer due
  Untaught to questions give,
Were't not that deep within the soul
  Truth's secret sparks do live?
If Plato's teaching erreth not,
We learn but that we have forgot.

* The doctrine of Reminiscence—*i.e.*, that all learning is really recollection—is set forth at length by Plato in the 'Meno,' 81-86, and the 'Phædo,' 72-76. See Jowett, vol. ii., pp. 40-47 and 213-218.

XII.

Then said I: 'With all my heart I agree with Plato; indeed, this is now the second time that these things have been brought back to my mind—first I lost them through the clogging contact of the body; then after through the stress of heavy grief.'

Then she continued: 'If thou wilt reflect upon thy former admissions, it will not be long before thou dost also recollect that of which erstwhile thou didst confess thyself ignorant.'

'What is that?' said I.

'The principles of the world's government,' said she.

'Yes; I remember my confession, and, although I now anticipate what thou intendest, I have a desire to hear the argument plainly set forth.'

'Awhile ago thou deemedst it beyond all doubt that God doth govern the world.'

'I do not think it doubtful now, nor

shall I ever; and by what reasons I am brought to this assurance I will briefly set forth. This world could never have taken shape as a single system out of parts so diverse and opposite were it not that there is One who joins together these so diverse things. And when it had once come together, the very diversity of natures would have dissevered it and torn it asunder in universal discord were there not One who keeps together what He has joined. Nor would the order of nature proceed so regularly, nor could its course exhibit motions so fixed in respect of position, time, range, efficacy, and character, unless there were One who, Himself abiding, disposed these various vicissitudes of change. This power, whatsoever it be, whereby they remain as they were created, and are kept in motion, I call by the name which all recognise—God.'

Then said she: 'Seeing that such is thy belief, it will cost me little trouble, I think, to enable thee to win happiness, and return in safety to thy own country. But let us give our attention to the task that we have set before ourselves. Have we not counted independence in the category of happiness, and agreed that God is absolute happiness?'

'Truly, we have.'

'Then, He will need no external assistance for the ruling of the world. Otherwise, if He stands in need of aught, He will not possess complete independence.'

'That is necessarily so,' said I.

'Then, by His own power alone He disposes all things.'

'It cannot be denied.'

'Now, God was proved to be absolute good.'

'Yes; I remember.'

'Then, He disposes all things by the agency of good, if it be true that *He* rules all things by His own power whom we have agreed to be good; and He is, as it were, the rudder and helm by which the world's mechanism is kept steady and in order.'

'Heartily do I agree; and, indeed, I anticipated what thou wouldst say, though it may be in feeble surmise only.'

'I well believe it,' said she; 'for, as I think, thou now bringest to the search eyes quicker in discerning truth; but what I shall say next is no less plain and easy to see.'

'What is it?' said I.

'Why,' said she, 'since God is rightly believed to govern all things with the rudder of goodness, and since all things do likewise, as I have taught, haste towards good by the very aim of nature, can it be doubted that His governance is willingly accepted, and that all submit themselves to the sway of the Disposer as conformed and attempered to His rule?'

'Necessarily so,' said I; 'no rule would seem happy if it were a yoke imposed on reluctant wills, and not the safe-keeping of obedient subjects.'

'There is nothing, then, which, while it follows nature, endeavours to resist good.'

'No; nothing.'

'But if anything should, will it have the least success against Him whom we rightly agreed to be supreme Lord of happiness?'

'It would be utterly impotent.'

'There is nothing, then, which has either the will or the power to oppose this supreme good.'

'No; I think not.'

'So, then,' said she, 'it is the supreme good which rules in strength, and graciously disposes all things.'

Then said I: 'How delighted am I at thy reasonings, and the conclusion to which thou hast brought them, but most of all at these very words which thou usest! I am now at last ashamed of the folly that so sorely vexed me.'

'Thou hast heard the story of the giants assailing heaven; but a beneficent strength disposed of them also, as they deserved. But shall we submit our arguments to the shock of mutual collision?—it may be from the impact some fair spark of truth may be struck out.'

'If it be thy good pleasure,' said I.

'No one can doubt that God is all-powerful.'

'No one at all can question it who thinks consistently.'

'Now, there is nothing which One who is all-powerful cannot do.'

'Nothing.'

'But can God do evil, then?'

'Nay; by no means.'

'Then, evil is nothing,' said she, 'since He to whom nothing is impossible is unable to do evil.'

'Art thou mocking me,' said I, 'weaving a labyrinth of tangled arguments, now seeming to begin where thou didst end, and now to end where thou didst begin, or dost thou build up some wondrous circle of Divine simplicity? For, truly, a little before thou didst begin with happiness, and say it was the supreme good, and didst declare it to be seated in the supreme Godhead. God Himself, too, thou didst affirm to be supreme good and all-complete happiness; and from this thou didst go on to add, as by the way, the proof that no one would be happy unless he were likewise God. Again, thou didst say that the very form of good was the essence both of God and of happiness, and didst teach that the absolute One was the absolute good which was sought by universal nature. Thou didst maintain, also, that God rules the universe by the governance of goodness, that all things obey Him willingly, and that evil has no existence in nature. And all this thou didst unfold without the help of assumptions from without, but by inherent and proper proofs, drawing credence one from the other.'

Then answered she: 'Far is it from me to mock thee; nay, by the blessing of God, whom we lately addressed in prayer, we have achieved the most important of all objects. For such is the form of the Divine essence, that neither can it pass into things external, nor take up anything external into itself; but, as Parmenides says of it,

> '"In body like to a sphere on all sides perfectly
> rounded,"

it rolls the restless orb of the universe, keeping itself motionless the while. And if I have also employed reasonings not drawn from without, but lying within the compass of our subject, there is no cause for thee to marvel, since thou hast learnt on Plato's authority that words ought to be akin to the matter of which they treat.'

SONG XII.

ORPHEUS AND EURYDICE.

Blest he whose feet have stood
Beside the fount of good;
Blest he whose will could break
Earth's chains for wisdom's sake!
The Thracian bard, 'tis said,
Mourned his dear consort dead;
To hear the plaintive strain
The woods moved in his train,
And the stream ceased to flow,
Held by so soft a woe;
The deer without dismay
Beside the lion lay;
The hound, by song subdued,
No more the hare pursued,
But the pang unassuaged
In his own bosom raged.
The music that could calm
All else brought him no balm.
Chiding the powers immortal,
He came unto Hell's portal;
There breathed all tender things
Upon his sounding strings,

Each rhapsody high-wrought
His goddess-mother taught—
All he from grief could borrow
And love redoubling sorrow,
Till, as the echoes waken,
All Tænarus is shaken;
Whilst he to ruth persuades
The monarch of the shades
With dulcet prayer. Spell-bound,
The triple-headed hound
At sounds so strangely sweet
Falls crouching at his feet.
The dread Avengers, too,
That guilty minds pursue
With ever-haunting fears,
Are all dissolved in tears.
Ixion, on his wheel,
A respite brief doth feel;
For, lo! the wheel stands still.
And, while those sad notes thrill,
Thirst-maddened Tantalus
Listens, oblivious
Of the stream's mockery
And his long agony.
The vulture, too, doth spare
Some little while to tear
At Tityus' rent side,
Sated and pacified.

At length the shadowy king,
His sorrows pitying,
'He hath prevailèd !' cried ;
'We give him back his bride !
To him she shall belong,
As guerdon of his song.
One sole condition yet
Upon the boon is set :
Let him not turn his eyes
To view his hard-won prize,
Till they securely pass
The gates of Hell.' Alas !
What law can lovers move ?
A higher law is love !
For Orpheus—woe is me !—
On his Eurydice—
Day's threshold all but won—
Looked, lost, and was undone !
Ye who the light pursue,
This story is for you,
Who seek to find a way
Unto the clearer day.
If on the darkness past
One backward look ye cast,
Your weak and wandering eyes
Have lost the matchless prize.

BOOK IV.

GOOD AND ILL FORTUNE.

SUMMARY.

Ch. I. The mystery of the seeming moral confusion. Philosophy engages to make this plain, and to fulfil her former promise to the full.—Ch. II. Accordingly, (*a*) she first expounds the paradox that the good alone have power, the bad are altogether powerless.—Ch. III. (*b*) The righteous never lack their reward, nor the wicked their punishment.—Ch. IV. (*c*) The wicked are more unhappy when they accomplish their desires than when they fail to attain them. (*d*) Evil-doers are more fortunate when they expiate their crimes by suffering punishment than when they escape unpunished. (*e*) The wrong-doer is more wretched than he who suffers injury.—Ch. V. Boethius still cannot understand why the distribution of happiness and misery to the righteous and the wicked seems the result of chance. Philosophy replies that this only seems so because we do not understand the principles of God's moral governance.—CH. VI. The distinction of Fate and Providence. The apparent moral confusion is due to our ignorance of the secret counsels of God's providence. If we possessed the key, we should see how all things are guided to good.—CH. VII. Thus all fortune is good fortune; for it either rewards, disciplines, amends, or punishes, and so is either useful or just.

BOOK IV.

I.

SOFTLY and sweetly Philosophy sang these verses to the end without losing aught of the dignity of her expression or the seriousness of her tones; then, forasmuch as I was as yet unable to forget my deeply-seated sorrow, just as she was about to say something further, I broke in and cried: 'O thou guide into the way of true light, all that thy voice hath uttered from the beginning even unto now has manifestly seemed to me at once divine contemplated in itself, and by the force of thy arguments placed beyond the possibility of overthrow. Moreover, these truths have not been altogether unfamiliar to me heretofore, though because of indignation at my wrongs they have for a time been forgotten. But, lo! herein is the very chiefest cause of my grief—that, while there exists a good ruler of the universe, it is possible that evil should be at all, still more that it should go unpunished. Surely thou must see how deservedly this of itself provokes astonishment. But a yet greater marvel follows: While wickedness reigns and flourishes, virtue not only lacks its reward, but is even thrust down and trampled under the feet of the wicked, and suffers punishment in the place of crime. That this should happen under the rule of a God who knows all things and can do all things, but wills only the good, cannot be sufficiently wondered at nor sufficiently lamented.'

Then said she: 'It would indeed be infinitely astounding, and of all monstrous things most horrible, if, as thou esteemest, in the well-ordered home of so great a householder, the base vessels should be held in honour, the precious left to neglect. But it is not so. For if we hold unshaken those conclusions which we lately reached, thou shalt learn that, by the will of Him of whose realm we are speaking, the good are always strong, the bad always weak and impotent ; that vices never go unpunished, nor virtues unrewarded ; that good fortune ever befalls the good, and ill fortune the bad, and much more of the sort, which shall hush thy murmurings, and stablish thee in the strong assurance of conviction. And since by my late instructions thou hast seen the form of happiness, hast learnt, too, the seat where it is to be found, all due preliminaries being discharged, I will now show thee the road which will lead thee home. Wings, also, will I fasten to thy mind wherewith thou mayst soar aloft, that so, all disturbing doubts removed, thou mayst return safe to thy country, under my guidance, in the path I will show thee, and by the means which I furnish.'

SONG I.

The Soul's Flight.

Wings are mine; above the pole
  Far aloft I soar.
Clothed with these, my nimble soul
  Scorns earth's hated shore,
Cleaves the skies upon the wind,
Sees the clouds left far behind.

Soon the glowing point she nears,
  Where the heavens rotate,
Follows through the starry spheres
  Phœbus' course, or straight
Takes for comrade 'mid the stars
Saturn cold or glittering Mars;

Thus each circling orb explores
  Through Night's stole that peers;
Then, when all are numbered, soars
  Far beyond the spheres,
Mounting heaven's supremest height
To the very Fount of light.

There the Sovereign of the world
  His calm sway maintains ;
As the globe is onward whirled
  Guides the chariot reins,
And in splendour glittering
Reigns the universal King.

Hither if thy wandering feet
  Find at last a way,
Here thy long-lost home thou'lt greet :
  'Dear lost land,' thou'lt say,
'Though from thee I've wandered wide,
Hence I came, here will abide.'

Yet if ever thou art fain
  Visitant to be
Of earth's gloomy night again,
  Surely thou wilt see
Tyrants whom the nations fear
Dwell in hapless exile here.

II.

Then said I: 'Verily, wondrous great are thy promises; yet I do not doubt but thou canst make them good: only keep me not in suspense after raising such hopes.'

'Learn, then, first,' said she, 'how that power ever waits upon the good, while the bad are left wholly destitute of strength.* Of these truths the one proves the other; for since good and evil are contraries, if it is made plain that good is power, the feebleness of evil is clearly seen, and, conversely, if the frail nature of evil is made manifest, the strength of good is thereby known. However, to win ampler credence for my conclusion, I will pursue both paths,

* The paradoxes in this chapter and chapter iv. are taken from Plato's 'Gorgias.' See Jowett, vol. ii., pp. 348-366, and also pp. 400, 401 ('Gorgias,' 466-479, and 508, 509).

and draw confirmation for my statements first in one way and then in the other.

'The carrying out of any human action depends upon two things—to wit, will and power; if either be wanting, nothing can be accomplished. For if the will be lacking, no attempt at all is made to do what is not willed; whereas if there be no power, the will is all in vain. And so, if thou seest any man wishing to attain some end, yet utterly failing to attain it, thou canst not doubt that he lacked the power of getting what he wished for.'

'Why, certainly not; there is no denying it.'

'Canst thou, then, doubt that he whom thou seest to have accomplished what he willed had also the power to accomplish it?'

'Of course not.'

'Then, in respect of what he can accomplish a man is to be reckoned strong, in respect of what he cannot accomplish weak?'

'Granted,' said I.

'Then, dost thou remember that, by our former reasonings, it was concluded that the whole aim of man's will, though the means of pursuit vary, is set intently upon happiness?'

'I do remember that this, too, was proved.'

'Dost thou also call to mind how happiness is absolute good, and therefore that, when happiness is sought, it is good which is in all cases the object of desire?'

'Nay, I do not so much call to mind as keep it fixed in my memory.'

'Then, all men, good and bad alike, with one indistinguishable purpose strive to reach good?'

'Yes, that follows.'

'But it is certain that by the attainment of good men become good?'

'It is.'

'Then, do the good attain their object?'

'It seems so.'

'But if the bad were to attain the good which is *their* object, they could not be bad?'

'No.'

'Then, since both seek good, but while the one sort attain it, the other attain it not, is there any doubt that the good are endued with power, while they who are bad are weak?'

'If any doubt it, he is incapable of reflecting on the nature of things, or the consequences involved in reasoning.'

'Again, supposing there are two things to which the same function is prescribed in the course of nature, and one of these successfully accomplishes the function by natural action, the other is altogether incapable of that natural action, instead of which, in a way other than is agreeable to its nature, it—I will not say fulfils its function, but feigns to fulfil it: which of these two would in thy view be the stronger?'

'I guess thy meaning, but I pray thee let me hear thee more at large.'

'Walking is man's natural motion, is it not?'

'Certainly.'

'Thou dost not doubt, I suppose, that it is natural for the feet to discharge this function?'

'No; surely I do not.'

'Now, if one man who is able to use his feet walks, and another to whom the natural use of his feet is wanting tries to walk on his hands, which of the two wouldst thou rightly esteem the stronger?'

'Go on,' said I; 'no one can question but that he who has the natural capacity has more strength than he who has it not.'

'Now, the supreme good is set up as the end alike for the bad and for the good; but the good seek it through the natural action of the virtues, whereas the bad try to attain this same good through all manner of concupiscence, which is not the natural way of attaining good. Or dost thou think otherwise?'

'Nay; rather, one further consequence is clear to me: for from my admissions it must needs follow that the good have power, and the bad are impotent.'

'Thou anticipatest rightly, and that as physicians reckon is a sign that nature is set working, and is throwing off the disease. But, since I see thee so ready at understanding, I will heap proof on proof. Look how manifest is the extremity of vicious men's weakness; they cannot even reach that goal to which the aim of nature leads and almost constrains them. What if they were left without this mighty, this well-nigh irresistible help of nature's guidance! Consider also how momentous is the powerlessness which incapacitates the wicked. Not light or trivial* are the prizes which they contend for, but which they cannot win or hold; nay, their failure concerns the very sum and crown of things. Poor wretches! they fail to compass even that for which they toil day and night. Herein also the strength of the good conspicuously appears. For just as thou wouldst judge him to be the strongest walker whose legs could carry him to a point beyond which no further advance was possible, so must thou needs account him strong in power who so attains the end of his desires that nothing further to be desired lies beyond. Whence follows the obvious conclusion that they who are wicked are seen likewise to be wholly

* 'No trivial game is here; the strife
Is waged for Turnus' own dear life.'
Conington.

See Virgil, 'Æneid,' xii. 764, 745: *cf.* 'Iliad,' xxii. 159-162.

destitute of strength. For why do they forsake virtue and follow vice? Is it from ignorance of what is good? Well, what is more weak and feeble than the blindness of ignorance? Do they know what they ought to follow, but lust drives them aside out of the way? If it be so, they are still frail by reason of their incontinence, for they cannot fight against vice. Or do they knowingly and wilfully forsake the good and turn aside to vice? Why, at this rate, they not only cease to have power, but cease to be at all. For they who forsake the common end of all things that are, they likewise also cease to be at all. Now, to some it may seem strange that we should assert that the bad, who form the greater part of mankind, do not exist. But the fact is so. I do not, indeed, deny that they who are bad are bad, but that they *are* in an unqualified and absolute sense I deny. Just as we call a corpse a dead man, but cannot call it simply "man," so I would allow the vicious to be bad, but that they *are* in an absolute sense I cannot allow. That only *is* which maintains its place and keeps its nature; whatever falls away from this forsakes the existence which is essential to its nature. "But," thou wilt say, "the bad have an ability." Nor do I wish to deny it; only this ability of theirs comes not from strength, but from impotence. For their ability is to do evil, which would have had no efficacy at all if they could have continued in the performance of good. So this ability of theirs proves them still more plainly to have no power. For if, as we concluded just now, evil is nothing, 'tis clear that the wicked can effect nothing, since they are only able to do evil.'

''Tis evident.'

'And that thou mayst understand what is the precise force of this power, we determined, did we not, awhile back, that nothing has more power than supreme good?'

'We did,' said I.

'But that same highest good cannot do evil?'

'Certainly not.'

'Is there anyone, then, who thinks that men are able to do all things?'

'None but a madman.'

'Yet they are able to do evil?'

'Ay; would they could not!'

'Since, then, he who can do only good is omnipotent, while they who can do evil also are not omnipotent, it is manifest that they who can do evil have less power. There is this also: we have shown that all power is to be reckoned among things desirable, and that all desirable things are referred to good as to a kind of consummation of their nature. But the ability to commit crime cannot be referred to the good; therefore it is not a thing to be desired. And yet all power is desirable; it is clear, then, that ability to do evil is not power. From all which considerations appeareth the power of the good, and the indubitable weakness of the bad, and it is clear that Plato's judgment was true; the wise alone are able to do what they would, while the wicked follow their own hearts' lust, but can *not* accomplish what they would. For they go on in their wilfulness fancying they will attain what they wish for in the paths of delight; but they are very far from its attainment, since shameful deeds lead not to happiness.'

SONG II.

THE BONDAGE OF PASSION.

When high-enthroned the monarch sits, resplendent in the pride
Of purple robes, while flashing steel guards him on every side;
When baleful terrors on his brow with frowning menace lower,
And Passion shakes his labouring breast—how dreadful seems his power!
But if the vesture of his state from such a one thou tear,
Thou'lt see what load of secret bonds this lord of earth doth wear.
Lust's poison rankles; o'er his mind rage sweeps in tempest rude;
Sorrow his spirit vexes sore, and empty hopes delude.
Then thou'lt confess: one hapless wretch, whom many lords oppress,
Does never what he would, but lives in thraldom's helplessness.

III.

'Thou seest, then, in what foulness unrighteous deeds are sunk, with what splendour righteousness shines. Whereby it is manifest that goodness never lacks its reward, nor crime its punishment. For, verily, in all manner of transactions that for the sake of which the particular action is done may justly be accounted the reward of that action, even as the wreath for the sake of which the race is run is the reward offered for running. Now, we have shown happiness to be that very good for the sake of which all things are done. Absolute good, then, is offered as the common prize, as it were, of all human actions. But, truly, this is a reward from which it is impossible to separate the good man, for one who is without good cannot properly be called good at all; wherefore righteous dealing never misses its reward. Rage the wicked, then, never so violently, the crown shall not fall from the head of the wise, nor wither. Verily, other men's unrighteousness cannot pluck from righteous souls their proper glory. Were the reward in which the soul of the righteous delighteth received from without, then might it be taken away by him who gave it, or some other; but since it is conferred by his own righteousness, then only will he lose his prize when he has ceased to be righteous. Lastly, since every prize is desired because it is believed to be good, who can account him who possesses good to be without reward? And what a prize, the fairest and grandest of all! For remember the corollary which I chiefly insisted on a little while back, and reason thus: Since absolute good is happiness, 'tis clear that all the good must be happy for the very reason that they are good. But it was agreed that those who are happy are gods. So, then, the prize of the good is one which no time may impair, no man's power lessen, no man's unrighteousness tarnish; 'tis very Godship. And this being so, the wise man cannot doubt that punishment is inseparable from the bad. For since good and bad, and likewise reward and punishment, are contraries, it necessarily follows that, corresponding to all that we see accrue as reward of the good, there is some penalty attached as punishment of evil. As, then, righteousness itself is the reward of the righteous, so wickedness itself is the punishment of the unrighteous. Now, no one who is visited with punishment doubts that he is visited with evil. Accordingly, if they were but willing to weigh their own case, could *they* think themselves free from punishment whom wickedness, worst of all evils, has not only touched, but deeply tainted?

'See, also, from the opposite standpoint the standpoint of the good—what a penalty attends upon the wicked. Thou didst learn a little since that whatever is is one, and that unity itself is good. Accordingly, by this way of reckoning, whatever falls away from goodness ceases to be; whence it comes to pass that the bad cease to be what they were, while only the outward aspect is still left to show they have been men. Wherefore, by their perversion to badness, they have lost their true human nature. Further, since righteousness alone can raise men above the level of humanity, it must needs be that unrighteousness degrades below man's level those whom it has cast out of man's estate. It results, then, that thou canst not consider him human whom thou seest transformed by vice. The violent despoiler of other men's goods, enflamed with covetousness, surely resembles a wolf. A bold and restless spirit, ever wrangling in law-courts, is like some yelping cur. The secret schemer, taking pleasure in fraud and stealth, is own brother to the fox. The passionate man, phrenzied with rage, we might believe to be animated with the soul of a lion. The coward and runaway, afraid where no fear is, may be likened to the timid deer. He who is sunk in ignorance and stupidity lives like a dull ass. He who is light and inconstant, never holding long to one thing, is for all the world like a bird. He who wallows in foul and unclean lusts is sunk in the pleasures of a filthy hog. So it comes to pass that he who by forsaking righteousness ceases to be a man cannot pass into a Godlike condition, but actually turns into a brute beast.'

SONG III.

Circe's Cup.

Th' Ithacan discreet,
And all his storm-tossed fleet,
Far o'er the ocean wave
The winds of heaven drave—
Drave to the mystic isle,
Where dwelleth in her guile
That fair and faithless one,
The daughter of the Sun.
There for the stranger crew
With cunning spells she knew
To mix th' enchanted cup.
For whoso drinks it up,
Must suffer hideous change
To monstrous shapes and strange.
One like a boar appears;
This his huge form uprears,
Mighty in bulk and limb—
An Afric lion—grim
With claw and fang. Confessed
A wolf, this, sore distressed
When he would weep, doth howl;
And, strangely tame, these prowl
The Indian tiger's mates.

And though in such sore straits,
The pity of the god
Who bears the mystic rod
Had power the chieftain brave
From her fell arts to save ;
His comrades, unrestrained,
The fatal goblet drained.
All now with low-bent head,
Like swine, on acorns fed ;
Man's speech and form were reft,
No human feature left ;
But steadfast still, the mind,
Unaltered, unresigned,
The monstrous change bewailed.
How little, then, availed
The potencies of ill !
These herbs, this baneful skill,
May change each outward part,
But cannot touch the heart.
In its true home, deep-set,
Man's spirit liveth yet.
Those poisons are more fell,
More potent to expel
Man from his high estate,
Which subtly penetrate,
And leave the body whole,
But deep infect the soul.

IV.

Then said I: 'This is very true. I see that the vicious, though they keep the outward form of man, are rightly said to be changed into beasts in respect of their spiritual nature; but, inasmuch as their cruel and polluted minds vent their rage in the destruction of the good, I would this license were not permitted to them.'

'Nor is it,' said she, 'as shall be shown in the fitting place. Yet if that license which thou believest to be permitted to them were taken away, the punishment of the wicked would be in great part remitted. For verily, incredible as it may seem to some, it needs must be that the bad are more unfortunate when they have accomplished their desires than if they are unable to get them fulfilled. If it is wretched to will evil, to have been able to accomplish evil is more wretched; for without the power the wretched will would fail of effect. Accordingly, those whom thou seest to will, to be able to accomplish, and to accomplish crime, must needs be the victims of a threefold wretchedness, since each one of these states has its own measure of wretchedness.'

'Yes,' said I; 'yet I earnestly wish they might speedily be quit of this misfortune by losing the ability to accomplish crime.'

'They will lose it,' said she, 'sooner than perchance thou wishest, or they themselves think likely; since, verily, within the narrow bounds of our brief life there is nothing so late in coming that anyone, least of all an immortal spirit, should deem it long to wait for. Their great expectations, the lofty fabric of their crimes, is oft overthrown by a sudden and unlooked-for ending, and this but sets a limit to their misery. For if wickedness makes men wretched, he is necessarily more wretched who is wicked for a longer time; and were it not that death, at all events, puts an end to the evil doings of the wicked, I should account them wretched to the last degree. Indeed, if we have formed true conclusions about the ill fortune of wickedness, that wretchedness is plainly infinite which is doomed to be eternal.'

Then said I: 'A wonderful inference, and difficult to grant; but I see that it agrees entirely with our previous conclusions.'

'Thou art right,' said she; 'but if anyone finds it hard to admit the conclusion, he ought in fairness either to prove some falsity in the premises, or to show that the combination of propositions does not adequately enforce the necessity of the conclusion; otherwise, if the premises be granted, nothing whatever can be said against the inference of the conclusion. And here is another statement which seems not less wonderful, but on the premises assumed is equally necessary.'

'What is that?'

'The wicked are happier in undergoing punishment than if no penalty of justice chasten them. And I am not now meaning what might occur to anyone—that bad character is amended by retribution, and is brought into the right path by the terror of punishment, or that it serves as an example to warn others to avoid transgression; but I believe that in another way the wicked are more unfortunate when they go unpunished, even though no account be taken of amendment, and no regard be paid to example.'

'Why, what other way is there beside these?' said I.

Then said she: 'Have we not agreed that the good are happy, and the evil wretched?'

'Yes,' said I.

'Now, if,' said she, 'to one in affliction there be given along with his misery some good thing, is he not happier than one whose misery is misery pure and simple without admixture of any good?'

'It would seem so.'

'But if to one thus wretched, one destitute of all good, some further evil be added besides those which make him wretched, is he not to be judged far more unhappy than he whose ill fortune is alleviated by some share of good?'

'It could scarcely be otherwise.'

'Surely, then, the wicked, when they are punished, have a good thing added to them—to wit, the punishment which by the law of justice is good; and likewise, when they escape punishment, a new evil attaches to them in that very freedom from punishment which thou hast rightly acknowledged to be an evil in the case of the unrighteous.'

'I cannot deny it.'

'Then, the wicked are far more unhappy when indulged with an unjust freedom from punishment than when punished by a just retribution. Now, it is manifest that it is just for the wicked to be punished, and for them to escape unpunished is unjust.'

'Why, who would venture to deny it?'

'This, too, no one can possibly deny—that all which is just is good, and, conversely, all which is unjust is bad.'

Then I answered: 'These inferences do indeed follow from what we lately concluded; but tell me,' said I, 'dost thou take no account of the punishment of the soul after the death of the body?'

'Nay, truly,' said she, 'great are these penalties, some of them inflicted, I imagine, in the severity of retribution, others in the mercy of purification. But it is not my present purpose to speak of these. So far, my aim hath been to make thee recognise that the power of the bad which shocked thee so exceedingly is no power; to make thee see that those of whose freedom from punishment thou didst complain are never without the proper penalties of their unrighteousness; to teach thee that the license which thou prayedst might soon come to an end is not long-enduring; that it would be more unhappy if it lasted longer, most unhappy of all if it lasted for ever; thereafter that the unrighteous are more wretched if unjustly let go without punishment than if punished by a just retribution—from which point of view it follows that the wicked are afflicted with more severe penalties just when they are supposed to escape punishment.'

Then said I: 'While I follow thy reasonings, I am deeply impressed with their truth; but if I turn to the common convictions of men, I find few who will even listen to such arguments, let alone admit them to be credible.'

'True,' said she; 'they cannot lift eyes accustomed to darkness to the light of clear truth, and are like those birds whose vision night illumines and day blinds; for while they regard, not the order of the universe, but their own dispositions of mind, they think the license to commit crime, and the escape from punishment, to be fortunate. But mark the ordinance of eternal law. Hast thou fashioned thy soul to the likeness of the better, thou hast no need of a judge to award the prize—by thine own act hast thou raised thyself in the scale of excellence; hast thou perverted thy affections to baser things, look not for punishment from one without thee—thine own act hath degraded thee, and thrust thee down. Even so, if alternately thou turn thy gaze upon the vile earth and upon the heavens, though all without thee stand still, by the mere laws of sight thou seemest now sunk in the mire, now soaring among the stars. But the common herd regards not these things. What, then? Shall we go over to those whom we have shown to be like brute beasts? Why, suppose, now, one who had quite lost his sight should likewise forget that he had ever possessed the faculty of vision, and should imagine that nothing was wanting in him to human perfection, should we deem those who saw as well as ever blind? Why, they will not even assent to this, either—that they who do wrong are more wretched than those who suffer wrong, though the proof of this rests on grounds of reason no less strong.'

'Let me hear these same reasons,' said I.

'Wouldst thou deny that every wicked man deserves punishment?'

'I would not, certainly.'

'And that those who are wicked are unhappy is clear in manifold ways?'

'Yes,' I replied.

'Thou dost not doubt, then, that those who deserve punishment are wretched?'

'Agreed,' said I.

'So, then, if thou wert sitting in judgment, on whom wouldst thou decree the infliction of punishment—on him who had done the wrong, or on him who had suffered it?'

'Without doubt, I would compensate the sufferer at the cost of the doer of the wrong.'

'Then, the injurer would seem more wretched than the injured?'

'Yes; it follows. And so for this and other reasons resting on the same ground, inasmuch as baseness of its own nature makes men wretched, it is plain that a wrong involves the misery of the doer, not of the sufferer.'

'And yet,' says she, 'the practice of the law-courts is just the opposite: advocates try to arouse the commiseration of the judges for those who have endured some grievous and cruel wrong; whereas pity is rather due to the criminal, who ought to be brought to the judgment-seat by his accusers in a spirit not of anger, but of compassion and kindness, as a sick man to the physician, to have the ulcer of his fault cut away by punishment. Whereby the business of the advocate would either wholly come to a standstill, or, did men prefer to make it serviceable to mankind, would be restricted to the practice of accusation. The wicked themselves also, if through some chink or cranny they were permitted to behold the virtue they have forsaken, and were to see that by the pains of punishment they would rid themselves of the uncleanness of their vices, and win in exchange the recompense of righteousness, they would no longer think these sufferings pains; they would refuse the help of advocates, and would commit themselves wholly into the hands of their accusers and judges. Whence it comes to pass that for the wise no place is left for hatred; only the most foolish would hate the good, and to hate the bad is unreasonable. For if vicious propensity is, as it were, a disease of the soul like bodily sickness, even as we account the sick in body by no means deserving of hate, but rather of pity, so, and much more, should they be pitied whose minds are assailed by wickedness, which is more frightful than any sickness.'

SONG IV.

The Unreasonableness of Hatred.

Why all this furious strife? Oh, why
With rash and wilful hand provoke death's destined day?
If death ye seek—lo! Death is nigh,
Not of their master's will those coursers swift delay!

The wild beasts vent on man their rage,
Yet 'gainst their brothers' lives men point the murderous steel;
Unjust and cruel wars they wage,
And haste with flying darts the death to meet or deal.

No right nor reason can they show;
'Tis but because their lands and laws are not the same.
Wouldst *thou* give each his due; then know
Thy love the good must have, the bad thy pity claim.

V.

On this I said: 'I see how there is a happiness and misery founded on the actual deserts of the righteous and the wicked. Nevertheless, I wonder in myself whether there is not some good and evil in fortune as the vulgar understand it. Surely, no sensible man would rather be exiled, poor and disgraced, than dwell prosperously in his own country, powerful, wealthy, and high in honour. Indeed, the work of wisdom is more clear and manifest in its operation when the happiness of rulers is somehow passed on to the people around them, especially considering that the prison, the law, and the other pains of legal punishment are properly due only to mischievous citizens on whose account they were originally instituted. Accordingly, I do exceedingly marvel why all this is completely reversed—why the good are harassed with the penalties due to crime, and the bad carry off the rewards of virtue; and I long to hear from thee what reason may be found for so unjust a state of disorder. For assuredly I should wonder less if I could believe that all things are the confused result of chance. But now my belief in God's governance doth add amazement to amazement. For, seeing that He sometimes assigns fair fortune to the good and harsh fortune to the bad, and then again deals harshly with the good, and grants to the bad their hearts' desire, how does this differ from chance, unless some reason is discovered for it all?'

'Nay; it is not wonderful,' said she, 'if all should be thought random and confused when the principle of order is not known. And though thou knowest not the causes on which this great system depends, yet forasmuch as a good ruler governs the world, doubt not for thy part that all is rightly done.'

SONG V.

Wonder and Ignorance.

Who knoweth not how near the pole
  Bootes' course doth go,
Must marvel by what heavenly law
  He moves his Wain so slow;
Why late he plunges 'neath the main,
And swiftly lights his beams again.

When the full-orbèd moon grows pale
  In the mid course of night,
And suddenly the stars shine forth
  That languished in her light,
Th' astonied nations stand at gaze,
And beat the air in wild amaze.*

None marvels why upon the shore
  The storm-lashed breakers beat,
Nor why the frost-bound glaciers melt
  At summer's fervent heat;
For here the cause seems plain and clear,
Only what's dark and hid we fear.

* To frighten away the monster swallowing the moon. The superstition was once common. See Tylor's 'Primitive Culture,' pp. 296-302.

Weak-minded folly magnifies
  All that is rare and strange,
And the dull herd's o'erwhelmed with awe
  At unexpected change.
But wonder leaves enlightened minds,
When ignorance no longer blinds.

VI.

'True,' said I; 'but, since it is thy office to unfold the hidden cause of things, and explain principles veiled in darkness, inform me, I pray thee, of thine own conclusions in this matter, since the marvel of it is what more than aught else disturbs my mind.'

A smile played one moment upon her lips as she replied: 'Thou callest me to the greatest of all subjects of inquiry, a task for which the most exhaustive treatment barely suffices. Such is its nature that, as fast as one doubt is cut away, innumerable others spring up like Hydra's heads, nor could we set any limit to their renewal did we not apply the mind's living fire to suppress them. For there come within its scope the questions of the essential simplicity of providence, of the order of fate, of unforeseen chance, of the Divine knowledge and predestination, and of the freedom of the will. How heavy is the weight of all this thou canst judge for thyself. But, inasmuch as to know these things also is part of the treatment of thy malady, we will try to give them some consideration, despite the restrictions of the narrow limits of our time. Moreover, thou must for a time dispense with the pleasures of music and song, if so be that thou findest any delight therein, whilst I weave together the connected train of reasons in proper order.'

'As thou wilt,' said I.

Then, as if making a new beginning, she thus discoursed: 'The coming into being of all things, the whole course of development in things that change, every sort of thing that moves in any wise, receives its due cause, order, and form from the steadfastness of the Divine mind. This mind, calm in the citadel of its own essential simplicity, has decreed that the method of its rule shall be manifold. Viewed in the very purity of the Divine intelligence, this method is called *providence*; but viewed in regard to those things which it moves and disposes, it is what the ancients called *fate*. That these two are different will easily be clear to anyone who passes in review their respective efficacies. Providence is the Divine reason itself, seated in the Supreme Being, which disposes all things; fate is the disposition inherent in all things which move, through which providence joins all things in their proper order. Providence embraces all things, however different, however infinite; fate sets in motion separately individual things, and assigns to them severally their position, form, and time.

'So the unfolding of this temporal order unified into the foreview of the Divine mind is providence, while the same unity broken up and unfolded in time is fate. And although these are different, yet is there a dependence between them; for the order of destiny issues from the essential simplicity of providence. For as the artificer, forming in his mind beforehand the idea of the thing to be made, carries out his design, and develops from moment to moment what he had before seen in a single instant as a whole, so God in His providence ordains all things as parts of a single unchanging whole, but carries out these very ordinances by fate in a time of manifold unity. So whether fate is accomplished by Divine spirits as the ministers of providence, or by a soul, or by the service of all nature—whether by the celestial motion of the stars, by the efficacy of angels, or by the many-sided cunning of demons—whether by all or by some of these the destined series is woven, this, at least, is manifest: that providence is the fixed and simple form of destined events, fate their shifting series in order of time, as by the disposal of the Divine simplicity they are to take place. Whereby it is that all things which are under fate are subjected also to providence, on which fate itself is dependent; whereas certain things which are set under providence are above the chain of fate—viz., those things which by their nearness to the primal Divinity are steadfastly fixed, and lie outside the order of fate's movements. For as the innermost of several circles revolving round the same centre approaches the simplicity of the midmost point, and is, as it were, a pivot round which the exterior circles turn, while the outermost, whirled in ampler orbit, takes in a wider and wider sweep of space in proportion to its departure from the indivisible unity of the centre—while, further, whatever joins and allies itself to the centre is narrowed to a like simplicity, and no longer expands vaguely into space—even so whatsoever departs widely from primal mind is involved more deeply in the meshes of fate, and things are free from fate in proportion as they seek to come nearer to that central pivot; while if aught cleaves close to supreme mind in its absolute fixity, this, too, being free from movement, rises above fate's necessity. Therefore, as is reasoning to pure intelligence, as that which is generated to that which is, time to eternity, a circle to its centre, so is the shifting series of fate to the steadfastness and simplicity of providence.

'It is this causal series which moves heaven and the stars, attempers the elements to mutual accord, and again in turn transforms them into new combinations; *this* which renews the series of all things that are born and die through like successions of germ and birth; it is *its* operation which binds the destinies of men by an indissoluble nexus of causality, and, since it issues in the beginning from unalterable providence, these destinies also must of necessity be immutable. Accordingly, the world is ruled for the best if this unity abiding in the Divine mind puts forth an inflexible order of causes. And this order, by its intrinsic immutability, restricts things mutable which otherwise would ebb and flow at random. And so it happens that, although to you, who are not altogether capable of understanding this order, all things seem confused and disordered, nevertheless there is everywhere an appointed limit which guides all things to good. Verily, nothing can be done for the sake of evil even by the wicked themselves; for, as we abundantly proved, they seek good, but are drawn out of the way by perverse error; far less can this order which sets out from the supreme centre of good turn aside anywhither from the way in which it began.

'"Yet what confusion," thou wilt say, "can be more unrighteous than that prosperity and adversity should indifferently befall the good, what they like and what they loathe come alternately to the bad!" Yes; but have men in real life such soundness of mind that their judgments of righteousness and wickedness must necessarily correspond with facts? Why, on this very point their verdicts conflict, and those whom some deem worthy of reward, others deem worthy of punishment. Yet granted there were one who could rightly distinguish the good and bad, yet would he be able to look into the soul's inmost constitution, as it were, if we may borrow an expression used of the body? The marvel here is not unlike that which astonishes one who does not know why in health sweet things suit some constitutions, and bitter others, or why some sick men are best alleviated by mild remedies, others by severe. But the physician who distinguishes the precise conditions and characteristics of health and sickness does not marvel. Now, the health of the soul is nothing but righteousness, and vice is its sickness. God, the guide and physician of the mind, it is who preserves the good and banishes the bad. And He looks forth from the lofty watch-tower of His providence, perceives what is suited to each, and assigns what He knows to be suitable.

'This, then, is what that extraordinary mystery of the order of destiny comes to—that something is done by one who knows, whereat the ignorant are astonished. But let us consider a few instances whereby appears what is the competency of human reason to fathom the Divine unsearchableness. Here is one whom thou deemest the perfection of justice and scrupulous integrity; to all-knowing Providence it seems far otherwise. We all know our Lucan's admonition that it was the winning cause that found favour with the gods, the beaten cause with Cato. So, shouldst thou see anything in this world happening differently from thy expectation, doubt not but events are rightly ordered; it is in thy judgment that there is perverse confusion.

'Grant, however, there be somewhere found one of so happy a character that God and man alike agree in their judgments about him; yet is he somewhat infirm in strength of mind. It may be, if he fall into adversity, he will cease to practise that innocency which has failed to secure his fortune. Therefore, God's wise dispensation spares him whom adversity might make worse, will not let him suffer who is ill fitted for endurance. Another there is perfect in all virtue, so holy and nigh to God that providence judges it unlawful that aught untoward should befall him; nay, doth not even permit him to be afflicted with bodily disease. As one more excellent than I* hath said:

> '"The very body of the holy saint
> Is built of purest ether."

Often it happens that the governance is given to the good that a restraint may be put upon superfluity of wickedness. To others providence assigns some mixed lot suited to their spiritual nature; some it will plague lest they grow rank through long prosperity; others it will suffer to be

* Parmenides. Boethius seems to forget for the moment that Philosophy is speaking.

vexed with sore afflictions to confirm their virtues by the exercise and practice of patience. Some fear overmuch what they have strength to bear; others despise overmuch that to which their strength is unequal. All these it brings to the test of their true self through misfortune. Some also have bought a name revered to future ages at the price of a glorious death; some by invincible constancy under their sufferings have afforded an example to others that virtue cannot be overcome by calamity—all which things, without doubt, come to pass rightly and in due order, and to the benefit of those to whom they are seen to happen.

'As to the other side of the marvel, that the bad now meet with affliction, now get their hearts' desire, this, too, springs from the same causes. As to the afflictions, of course no one marvels, because all hold the wicked to be ill deserving. The truth is, their punishments both frighten others from crime, and amend those on whom they are inflicted; while their prosperity is a powerful sermon to the good, what judgments they ought to pass on good fortune of this kind, which often attends the wicked so assiduously.

'There is another object which may, I believe, be attained in such cases: there is one, perhaps, whose nature is so reckless and violent that poverty would drive him more desperately into crime. *His* disorder providence relieves by allowing him to amass money. Such a one, in the uneasiness of a conscience stained with guilt, while he contrasts his character with his fortune, perchance grows alarmed lest he should come to mourn the loss of that whose possession is so pleasant to him. He will, then, reform his ways, and through the fear of losing his fortune he forsakes his iniquity. Some, through a prosperity unworthily borne, have been hurled headlong to ruin; to some the power of the sword has been committed, to the end that the good may be tried by discipline, and the bad punished. For while there can be no peace between the righteous and the wicked, neither can the wicked agree among themselves. How should they, when each is at variance with himself, because his vices rend his conscience, and ofttimes they do things which, when they are done, they judge ought not to have been done. Hence it is that this supreme providence brings to pass this notable marvel—that the bad make the bad good. For some, when they see the injustice which they themselves suffer at the hands of evil-doers, are inflamed with detestation of the offenders, and, in the endeavour to be unlike those whom they hate, return to the ways of virtue. It is the Divine power alone to which things evil are also good, in that, by putting them to suitable use, it bringeth them in the end to some good issue. For order in some way or other embraceth all things, so that even that which has departed from the appointed laws of the order, nevertheless falleth within *an* order, though *another* order, that nothing in the realm of providence may be left to haphazard. But

'"Hard were the task, as a god, to recount all, nothing omitting."

Nor, truly, is it lawful for man to compass in thought all the mechanism of the Divine work, or set it forth in speech. Let us be content to have apprehended this only—that God, the creator of universal nature, likewise disposeth all things, and guides them to good; and while He studies to preserve in likeness to Himself all that He has created, He banishes all evil from the borders of His commonweal through the links of fatal necessity. Whereby it comes to pass that, if thou look to disposing providence, thou wilt nowhere find the evils which are believed so to abound on earth.

'But I see thou hast long been burdened with the weight of the subject, and fatigued with the prolixity of the argument, and now lookest for some refreshment of sweet poesy. Listen, then, and may the draught so restore thee that thou wilt bend thy mind more resolutely to what remains.'

SONG VI.

The Universal Aim.

Wouldst thou with unclouded mind
View the laws by God designed,
Lift thy steadfast gaze on high
To the starry canopy;
See in rightful league of love
All the constellations move.
Fiery Sol, in full career,
Ne'er obstructs cold Phœbe's sphere;
When the Bear, at heaven's height,
Wheels his coursers' rapid flight,
Though he sees the starry train
Sinking in the western main,
He repines not, nor desires
In the flood to quench his fires.
In true sequence, as decreed,
Daily morn and eve succeed;
Vesper brings the shades of night,
Lucifer the morning light.
Love, in alternation due,
Still the cycle doth renew,
And discordant strife is driven
From the starry realm of heaven.

Thus, in wondrous amity,
Warring elements agree ;
Hot and cold, and moist and dry,
Lay their ancient quarrel by ;
High the flickering flame ascends,
Downward earth for ever tends.
  So the year in spring's mild hours
Loads the air with scent of flowers ;
Summer paints the golden grain ;
Then, when autumn comes again,
Bright with fruit the orchards glow ;
Winter brings the rain and snow.
Thus the seasons' fixed progression,
Tempered in a due succession,
Nourishes and brings to birth
All that lives and breathes on earth.
Then, soon run life's little day,
All it brought it takes away.
  But One sits and guides the reins,
He who made and all sustains ;
King and Lord and Fountain-head,
Judge most holy, Law most dread ;
Now impels and now keeps back,
Holds each waverer in the track.
Else, were once the power withheld
That the circling spheres compelled

In their orbits to revolve,
This world's order would dissolve,
And th' harmonious whole would all
In one hideous ruin fall.
  But through this connected frame
Runs one universal aim ;
Towards the Good do all things tend,
Many paths, but one the end.
For naught lasts, unless it turns
Backward in its course, and yearns
To that Source to flow again
Whence its being first was ta'en.

VII.

'Dost thou, then, see the consequence of all that we have said?'

'Nay; what consequence?'

'That absolutely every fortune is good fortune.'

'And how can that be?' said I.

'Attend,' said she. 'Since every fortune, welcome and unwelcome alike, has for its object the reward or trial of the good, and the punishing or amending of the bad, every fortune must be good, since it is either just or useful.'

'The reasoning is exceeding true,' said I, 'the conclusion, so long as I reflect upon the providence and fate of which thou hast taught me, based on a strong foundation. Yet, with thy leave, we will count it among those which just now thou didst set down as paradoxical.'

'And why so?' said she.

'Because ordinary speech is apt to

assert, and that frequently, that some men's fortune is bad.'

'Shall we, then, for awhile approach more nearly to the language of the vulgar, that we may not seem to have departed too far from the usages of men?'

'At thy good pleasure,' said I.

'That which advantageth thou callest good, dost thou not?'

'Certainly.'

'And that which either tries or amends advantageth?'

'Granted.'

'Is good, then?'

'Of course.'

'Well, this is *their* case who have attained virtue and wage war with adversity, or turn from vice and lay hold on the path of virtue.'

'I cannot deny it.'

'What of the good fortune which is given as reward of the good—do the vulgar adjudge it bad?'

'Anything but that; they deem it to be the best, as indeed it is.'

'What, then, of that which remains, which, though it is harsh, puts the restraint of just punishment on the bad—does popular opinion deem it good?'

'Nay; of all that can be imagined, it is accounted the most miserable.'

'Observe, then, if, in following popular opinion, we have not ended in a conclusion quite paradoxical.'

'How so?' said I.

'Why, it results from our admissions that of all who have attained, or are advancing in, or are aiming at virtue, the fortune is in every case good, while for those who remain in their wickedness fortune is always utterly bad.'

'It is true,' said I; 'yet no one dare acknowledge it.'

'Wherefore,' said she, 'the wise man ought not to take it ill, if ever he is involved in one of fortune's conflicts, any more than it becomes a brave soldier to be offended when at any time the trumpet sounds for battle. The time of trial is the express opportunity for the one to win glory, for the other to perfect his wisdom. Hence, indeed, virtue gets its name, because, relying on its own efficacy, it yieldeth not to adversity. And ye who have taken your stand on virtue's steep ascent, it is not for you to be dissolved in delights or enfeebled by pleasure; ye close in conflict—yea, in conflict most sharp—with all fortune's vicissitudes, lest ye suffer foul fortune to overwhelm or fair fortune to corrupt you. Hold the mean with all your strength. Whatever falls short of this, or goes beyond, is fraught with scorn of happiness, and misses the reward of toil. It rests with you to make your fortune what you will. Verily, every harsh-seeming fortune, unless it either disciplines or amends, is punishment.'

SONG VII.

THE HERO'S PATH.

Ten years a tedious warfare raged,
  Ere Ilium's smoking ruins paid
  For wedlock stained and faith betrayed,
And great Atrides' wrath assuaged.

But when heaven's anger asked a life,
  And baffling winds his course withstood,
  The king put off his fatherhood,
And slew his child with priestly knife.

When by the cavern's glimmering light
  His comrades dear Odysseus saw
  In the huge Cyclops' hideous maw
Engulfed, he wept the piteous sight.

But blinded soon, and wild with pain—
  In bitter tears and sore annoy—
  For that foul feast's unholy joy
Grim Polyphemus paid again.

His labours for Alcides win
  A name of glory far and wide ;
  He tamed the Centaur's haughty pride,
And from the lion reft his skin.

The foul birds with sure darts he slew;
  The golden fruit he stole—in vain
  The dragon's watch; with triple chain
From hell's depths Cerberus he drew.

With their fierce lord's own flesh he fed
  The wild steeds; Hydra overcame
  With fire. 'Neath his own waves in shame
Maimed Achelous hid his head.

Huge Cacus for his crimes was slain;
  On Libya's sands Antæus hurled;
  The shoulders that upheld the world
The great boar's dribbled spume did stain.

Last toil of all—his might sustained
  The ball of heaven, nor did he bend
  Beneath; this toil, his labour's end,
The prize of heaven's high glory gained.

Brave hearts, press on! Lo, heavenward lead
  These bright examples! From the fight
  Turn not your backs in coward flight;
Earth's conflict won, the stars your meed!

BOOK V.

FREE WILL AND GOD'S FOREKNOWLEDGE.

SUMMARY.

CH. I. Boethius asks if there is really any such thing as chance. Philosophy answers, in conformity with Aristotle's definition (Phys., II. iv.), that chance is merely relative to human purpose, and that what seems fortuitous really depends on a more subtle form of causation.—CH. II. Has man, then, any freedom, if the reign of law is thus absolute? Freedom of choice, replies Philosophy, is a necessary attribute of reason. Man has a measure of freedom, though a less perfect freedom than divine natures.—CH. III. But how can man's freedom be reconciled with God's absolute foreknowledge? If God's foreknowledge be certain, it seems to exclude the possibility of man's free will. But if man has no freedom of choice, it follows that rewards and punishments are unjust as well as useless; that merit and demerit are mere names; that God is the cause of men's wickednesses; that prayer is meaningless.—CH. IV. The explanation is that man's reasoning faculties are not adequate to the apprehension of the ways of God's foreknowledge. If we could know, as He knows, all that is most perplexing in this problem would be made plain. For knowledge depends not on the nature of the thing known, but on the faculty of the knower.—CH. V. Now, where our senses conflict with our reason, we defer the judgment of the lower faculty to the judgment of the higher. Our present perplexity arises from our viewing God's foreknowledge from the standpoint of human reason. We must try and rise to the higher standpoint of God's immediate intuition.—CH. VI. To understand this higher form of cognition, we must consider God's nature. God is eternal. Eternity is more than mere everlasting duration. Accordingly, His knowledge surveys past and future in the timelessness of an eternal present. His foreseeing is seeing. Yet this foreseeing does not in itself impose necessity, any more than our seeing things happen makes their happening necessary. We may, however, if we please, distinguish two necessities—one absolute, the other conditional on knowledge. In this conditional sense alone do the things which God foresees necessarily come to pass. But this kind of necessity affects not the nature of things. It leaves the reality of free will unimpaired, and the evils feared do not ensue. Our responsibility is great, since all that we do is done in the sight of all-seeing Providence.

BOOK V.

I.

SHE ceased, and was about to pass on in her discourse to the exposition of other matters, when I break in and say: 'Excellent is thine exhortation, and such as well beseemeth thy high authority; but I am even now experiencing one of the many difficulties which, as thou saidst but now, beset the question of providence. I want to know whether thou deemest that there is any such thing as chance at all, and, if so, what it is.'

Then she made answer: 'I am anxious to fulfil my promise completely, and open to thee a way of return to thy native land. As for these matters, though very useful to know, they are yet a little removed from the path of our design, and I fear lest digressions should fatigue thee, and thou shouldst find thyself unequal to completing the direct journey to our goal.'

'Have no fear for that,' said I. 'It is rest to me to learn, where learning brings delight so exquisite, especially when thy argument has been built up on all sides with undoubted conviction, and no place is left for uncertainty in what follows.'

She made answer: 'I will accede to thy request;' and forthwith she thus began: 'If chance be defined as a result produced by random movement without any link of causal connection, I roundly affirm that there is no such thing as chance at all, and consider the word to be altogether without meaning, except as a symbol of the thing designated. What place can be left for random action, when God constraineth all things to order? For "ex nihilo nihil" is sound doctrine which none of the ancients gainsaid, although they used it of material substance, not of the efficient principle; this they laid down as a kind of basis for all their reasonings concerning nature. Now, if a thing arise without causes, it will appear to have arisen from nothing. But if this cannot be, neither is it possible for there to be chance in accordance with the definition just given.'

'Well,' said I, 'is there, then, nothing which can properly be called chance or accident, or is there something to which these names are appropriate, though its nature is dark to the vulgar?'

'Our good Aristotle,' says she, 'has defined it concisely in his "Physics," and closely in accordance with the truth.'

'How, pray?' said I.

'Thus,' says she: 'Whenever something is done for the sake of a particular end, and for certain reasons some other result than that designed ensues, this is called chance; for instance, if a man is digging the earth for tillage, and finds a mass of buried gold. Now, such a find is regarded as accidental; yet it is not "ex nihilo," for it has its proper causes, the unforeseen and unexpected concurrence of which has brought the chance about. For had not the cultivator been digging, had not the man who hid the money buried it in that precise spot, the gold would not have been found. These, then, are the reasons why the find is a chance one, in that it results from causes which met together and concurred, not from any intention on the part of the discoverer. Since neither he who buried the gold nor he who worked in the field *intended* that the money should be found, but, as I said, it *happened* by coincidence that one dug where the other buried the treasure. We may, then, define chance as being an unexpected result flowing from a concurrence of causes where the several factors had some definite end. But the meeting and concurrence of these causes arises from that inevitable chain of order which, flowing from the fountain-head of Providence, disposes all things in their due time and place.'

SONG I.

Chance.

In the rugged Persian highlands,
  Where the masters of the bow
Skill to feign a flight, and, fleeing,
  Hurl their darts and pierce the foe;
There the Tigris and Euphrates
  At one source* their waters blend,
Soon to draw apart, and plainward
  Each its separate way to wend.
When once more their waters mingle
  In a channel deep and wide,
All the flotsam comes together
  That is borne upon the tide:
Ships, and trunks of trees, uprooted
  In the torrent's wild career,
Meet, as 'mid the swirling waters
  Chance their random way may steer.

* This is not, of course, literally true, though the Tigris and Euphrates rise in the same mountain district.

Yet the shelving of the channel
  And the flowing water's force
Guides each movement, and determines
  Every floating fragment's course.
Thus, where'er the drift of hazard
  Seems most unrestrained to flow,
Chance herself is reined and bitted,
  And the curb of law doth know.

II.

'I am following heedfully,' said I, 'and I agree that it is as thou sayest. But in this series of linked causes is there any freedom left to our will, or does the chain of fate bind also the very motions of our souls?'

'There is freedom,' said she; 'nor, indeed, can any creature be rational, unless he be endowed with free will. For that which hath the natural use of reason has the faculty of discriminative judgment, and of itself distinguishes what is to be shunned or desired. Now, everyone seeks what he judges desirable, and avoids what he thinks should be shunned. Wherefore, beings endowed with reason possess also the faculty of free choice and refusal. But I suppose this faculty not equal alike in all. The higher Divine essences possess a clear-sighted judgment, an uncorrupt will, and an effective power of accomplishing their wishes. Human souls must needs be comparatively free while they abide in the contemplation of the Divine mind, less free when they pass into bodily form, and still less, again, when they are enwrapped in earthly members. But when they are given over to vices, and fall from the possession of their proper reason, then indeed their condition is utter slavery. For when they let their gaze fall from the light of highest truth to the lower world where darkness reigns, soon ignorance blinds their vision; they are disturbed by baneful affections, by yielding and assenting to which they help to promote the slavery in which they are involved, and are in a manner led captive by reason of their very liberty. Yet He who seeth all things from eternity beholdeth these things with the eyes of His providence, and assigneth to each what is predestined for it by its merits:

'"All things surveying, all things overhearing."'

SONG II.

THE TRUE SUN.

Homer with mellifluous tongue
Phœbus' glorious light hath sung,
  Hymning high his praise;
  Yet *his* feeble rays
Ocean's hollows may not brighten,
Nor earth's central gloom enlighten.

But the might of Him, who skilled
This great universe to build,
  Is not thus confined;
  Not earth's solid rind,
Nor night's blackest canopy,
Baffle His all-seeing eye.

All that is, hath been, shall be,
In one glance's compass, He
  Limitless descries;
  And, save His, no eyes
All the world survey—no, none!
Him, then, truly name the Sun.

III.

Then said I: 'But now I am once more perplexed by a problem yet more difficult.'

'And what is that?' said she; 'yet, in truth, I can guess what it is that troubles you.'

'It seems,' said I, 'too much of a paradox and a contradiction that God should know all things, and yet there should be free will. For if God foresees everything, and can in no wise be deceived, that which providence foresees to be about to happen must necessarily come to pass. Wherefore, if from eternity He foreknows not only what men will do, but also their designs and purposes, there can be no freedom of the will, seeing that nothing can be done, nor can any sort of purpose be entertained, save such as a Divine providence, incapable of being deceived, has perceived beforehand. For if the issues can be turned aside to some other end than that foreseen by providence, there will not then be any sure foreknowledge of the future, but uncertain conjecture instead, and to think this of God I deem impiety.

'Moreover, I do not approve the reasoning by which some think to solve this puzzle. For they say that it is not because God has foreseen the coming of an event that *therefore* it is sure to come to pass, but, conversely, because something is about to come to pass, it cannot be hidden from Divine providence; and accordingly the necessity passes to the opposite side, and it is not that what is foreseen must necessarily come to pass, but that what is about to come to pass must necessarily be foreseen. But this is just as if the matter in debate were, which is cause and which effect — whether foreknowledge of the future cause of the necessity, or the necessity of the future of the foreknowledge. But we need not be at the pains of demonstrating that, whatsoever be the order of the causal sequence, the occurrence of things foreseen is necessary, even though the foreknowledge of future events does not in itself impose upon them the necessity of their occurrence. For example, if a man be seated, the supposition of his being seated is necessarily true; and, conversely, if the supposition of his being seated is true, because he is really seated, he must necessarily be sitting. So, in either case, there is some necessity involved—in this latter case, the necessity of the fact; in the former, of the truth of the statement. But in both cases the sitter is not therefore seated because the opinion is true, but rather the opinion is true because antecedently he was sitting as a matter of fact. Thus, though the cause of the truth of the opinion comes from the other side,* yet there is a necessity on both sides alike. We can obviously reason similarly in the case of providence and the future. Even if future events are foreseen because they are about to happen, and do not come to pass because they are foreseen, still, all the same, there is a necessity, both that they should be fore-

* *I.e.*, the necessity of the truth of the statement from the fact.

seen by God as about to come to pass, and that when they are foreseen they should happen, and this is sufficient for the destruction of free will. However, it is preposterous to speak of the occurrence of events in time as the cause of eternal foreknowledge. And yet if we believe that God foresees future events because they are about to come to pass, what is it but to think that the occurrence of events is the cause of His supreme providence? Further, just as when I *know* that anything is, that thing *necessarily* is, so when I know that anything will be, it will *necessarily* be. It follows, then, that things foreknown come to pass inevitably.

'Lastly, to think of a thing as being in any way other than what it is, is not only not knowledge, but it is false opinion widely different from the truth of knowledge. Consequently, if anything is about to be, and yet its occurrence is not certain and necessary, how can anyone foreknow that it will occur? For just as knowledge itself is free from all admixture of falsity, so any conception drawn from knowledge cannot be other than as it is conceived.

For this, indeed, is the cause why knowledge is free from falsehood, because of necessity each thing must correspond exactly with the knowledge which grasps its nature. In what way, then, are we to suppose that God foreknows these uncertainties as about to come to pass? For if He thinks of events which possibly may not happen at all as inevitably destined to come to pass, He is deceived; and this it is not only impious to believe, but even so much as to express in words. If, on the other hand, He sees them in the future as they are in such a sense as to know that they may equally come to pass or not, what sort of foreknowledge is this which comprehends nothing certain nor fixed? What better is this than the absurd vaticination of Teiresias?

> '"Whate'er I say
> Shall either come to pass—or not."

In that case, too, in what would Divine providence surpass human opinion if it holds for uncertain things the occurrence of which is uncertain, even as men do? But if at that perfectly sure Fountain-head of all things no shadow of uncertainty can possibly be found, then the occurrence of those things which He has surely foreknown as coming is certain. Wherefore there can be no freedom in human actions and designs; but the Divine mind, which foresees all things without possibility of mistake, ties and binds them down to one only issue. But this admission once made, what an upset of human affairs manifestly ensues! Vainly are rewards and punishments proposed for the good and bad, since no free and voluntary motion of the will has deserved either one or the other; nay, the punishment of the wicked and the reward of the righteous, which is now esteemed the perfection of justice, will seem the most flagrant injustice, since men are determined either way not by their own proper volition, but by the necessity of what must surely be. And therefore neither virtue nor vice is anything, but rather good and ill desert are confounded together without distinction. Moreover, seeing that the whole course of events is deduced from providence, and nothing is left free to human design, it comes to pass that our vices also are referred to the Author of all good—a thought than which none more abominable can possibly be conceived. Again, no ground is left for hope or prayer, since how can we hope for blessings, or pray for mercy, when every object of desire depends upon the links of an unalterable chain of causation? Gone, then, is the one means of intercourse between God and man—the communion of hope and prayer—if it be true that we ever earn the inestimable recompense of the Divine favour at the price of a due humility; for this is the one way whereby men seem able to hold communion with God, and are joined to that unapproachable light by the very act of supplication, even before they obtain their petitions. Then, since these things can scarcely be believed to have any efficacy, if the necessity of future events be admitted, what means will there be whereby we may be brought near and cleave to Him who is the supreme Head of all? Wherefore it needs must be that the human race, even as thou didst erstwhile declare in song, parted and dissevered from its Source, should fall to ruin.'

SONG III.

Truth's Paradoxes.

Why does a strange discordance break
  The ordered scheme's fair harmony?
Hath God decreed 'twixt truth and truth
  There may such lasting warfare be,
That truths, each severally plain,
We strive to reconcile in vain?

Or is the discord not in truth,
  Since truth is self-consistent ever?
But, close in fleshly wrappings held,
  The blinded mind of man can never
Discern—so faint her taper shines—
The subtle chain that all combines?

Ah! then why burns man's restless mind
  Truth's hidden portals to unclose?
Knows he already what he seeks?
  Why toil to seek it, if he knows?
Yet, haply if he knoweth not,
Why blindly seek he knows not what?*

* Compare Plato, 'Meno,' 80; Jowett, vol. ii., pp. 39, 40.

Who for a good he knows not sighs?
  Who can an unknown end pursue?
How find? How e'en when haply found
  Hail that strange form he never knew?
Or is it that man's inmost soul
Once knew each part and knew the whole?

Now, though by fleshly vapours dimmed,
  Not all forgot her visions past;
For while the several parts are lost,
  To the one whole she cleaveth fast;
Whence he who yearns the truth to find
Is neither sound of sight nor blind.

For neither does he know in full,
  Nor is he reft of knowledge quite;
But, holding still to what is left,
  He gropes in the uncertain light,
And by the part that still survives
To win back all he bravely strives.

IV.

Then said she: 'This debate about providence is an old one, and is vigorously discussed by Cicero in his "Divination"; thou also hast long and earnestly pondered the problem, yet no one has had diligence and perseverance enough to find a solution. And the reason of this obscurity is that the movement of human reasoning cannot cope with the simplicity of the Divine foreknowledge; for if a conception of its nature could in any wise be framed, no shadow of uncertainty would remain. With a view of making this at last clear and plain, I will begin by considering the arguments by which thou art swayed. First, I inquire into the reasons why thou art dissatisfied with the solution proposed, which is to the effect that, seeing the fact of foreknowledge is not thought the cause of the necessity of future events, foreknowledge is not to be deemed any hindrance to the freedom of the will.

Now, surely the sole ground on which thou arguest the necessity of the future is that things which are foreknown cannot fail to come to pass. But if, as thou wert ready to acknowledge just now, the fact of foreknowledge imposes no necessity on things future, what reason is there for supposing the results of voluntary action constrained to a fixed issue? Suppose, for the sake of argument, and to see what follows, we assume that there is no foreknowledge. Are willed actions, then, tied down to any necessity in *this* case?'

'Certainly not.'

'Let us assume foreknowledge again, but without its involving any actual necessity; the freedom of the will, I imagine, will remain in complete integrity. But thou wilt say that, even although the foreknowledge is not the necessity of the future event's occurrence, yet it is a sign that it will necessarily happen. Granted; but in this case it is plain that, even if there had been no foreknowledge, the issues would have been inevitably certain. For a sign only indicates something which is, does not bring to pass that of which it is the sign. We require to show beforehand that all things, without exception, happen of necessity in order that a preconception may be a sign of this necessity. Otherwise, if there is no such universal necessity, neither can any preconception be a sign of a necessity which exists not. Manifestly, too, a proof established on firm grounds of reason must be drawn not from signs and loose general arguments, but from suitable and necessary causes. But how can it be that things foreseen should ever fail to come to pass? Why, this is to suppose us to believe that the events which providence foresees to be coming were not about to happen, instead of our supposing that, although they should come to pass, yet there was no necessity involved in their own nature compelling their occurrence. Take an illustration that will help to convey my meaning. There are many things which we see taking place before our eyes — the movements of charioteers, for instance, in guiding and turning their cars, and so on. Now, is any one of these movements compelled by any necessity?'

'No; certainly not. There would be no efficacy in skill if all motions took place perforce.'

'Then, things which in taking place are free from any necessity as to their being in the present must also, before they take place, be about to happen without necessity. Wherefore there are things which will come to pass, the occurrence of which is perfectly free from necessity. At all events, I imagine that no one will deny that things now taking place were about to come to pass before they were actually happening. Such things, however much foreknown, are in their occurrence *free.* For even as knowledge of things present imports no necessity into things that are taking place, so foreknowledge of the future imports none into things that are about to come. But this, thou wilt say, is the very point in dispute—whether any foreknowing is possible of things whose occurrence is not necessary. For here there seems to thee a contradiction, and, if they are foreseen, their necessity follows; whereas if there is no necessity, they can by no means be foreknown; and thou thinkest that nothing can be grasped as known unless it is certain, but if things whose occurrence is uncertain are foreknown as certain, this is the very mist of opinion, not the truth of knowledge. For to think of things otherwise than as they are, thou believest to be incompatible with the soundness of knowledge.

'Now, the cause of the mistake is this—that men think that all knowledge is cognized purely by the nature and efficacy of the thing known. Whereas the case is the very reverse: all that is known is grasped not conformably to its own efficacy, but rather conformably to the faculty of the knower. An example will make this clear: the roundness of a body is recognised in one way by sight, in another by touch. Sight looks upon it from a distance as a whole by a simultaneous reflection of rays; touch grasps the roundness piecemeal, by contact and attachment to the surface, and by actual movement round the periphery itself. Man himself, likewise, is viewed in one way by Sense, in another by Imagination, in another way, again, by Thought, in another by pure Intelligence. Sense judges figure clothed in material substance, Imagination figure alone without matter. Thought transcends this again, and by its contemplation of universals considers the type itself which is contained in the individual. The eye of Intelligence is yet more exalted; for overpassing the sphere of the universal, it will behold absolute form itself by the pure force of the mind's vision. Wherein the main point to be considered is this: the higher faculty of comprehension embraces the lower, while the lower cannot rise to the higher. For Sense has no efficacy beyond matter, nor can Imagination behold universal ideas, nor Thought embrace pure form; but Intelligence, looking down, as it were, from its higher standpoint in its intuition of form, discriminates also the several elements which underlie it; but it comprehends them in the same way as it comprehends that form itself, which could be cognized by no other than itself. For it cognizes the universal of Thought, the figure of Imagination, and the matter of Sense, without employing Thought, Imagination, or Sense, but surveying all things, so to speak, under the aspect of pure form by a single flash of intuition. Thought also, in considering the universal, embraces images and sense-impressions without resorting to Imagination or Sense. For it is Thought which has thus defined the universal from its conceptual point of view: "Man is a two-legged animal endowed with reason." This is indeed a universal notion, yet no one is ignorant that the *thing* is imaginable and presentable to Sense, because Thought considers it not by Imagination or Sense, but by means of rational conception. Imagination, too, though its faculty of viewing and forming representations is founded upon the senses, nevertheless surveys sense-impressions without calling in Sense, not in the way of Sense-perception, but of Imagination. See'st thou, then, how all things in cognizing use rather their own faculty than the faculty of the things which they cognize? Nor is this strange; for since every judgment is the act of the judge, it is necessary that each should accomplish its task by its own, not by another's power.'

SONG IV.

A PSYCHOLOGICAL FALLACY.*

From the Porch's murky depths
  Comes a doctrine sage,
That doth liken living mind
  To a written page;
Since all knowledge comes through
    Sense,
Graven by Experience.

'As,' say they, 'the pen its marks
  Curiously doth trace
On the smooth unsullied white
  Of the paper's face,
So do outer things impress
Images on consciousness.'

But if verily the mind
  Thus all passive lies;
If no living power within
  Its own force supplies;
If it but reflect again,
Like a glass, things false and vain—

* A criticism of the doctrine of the mind as a blank sheet of paper on which experience writes, as held by the Stoics in anticipation of Locke. See Zeller, 'Stoics, Epicureans, and Sceptics,' Reichel's translation, p. 76.

Whence the wondrous faculty
  That perceives and knows,
That in one fair ordered scheme
  Doth the world dispose;
Grasps each whole that Sense presents,
Or breaks into elements?

So divides and recombines,
  And in changeful wise
Now to low descends, and now
  To the height doth rise;
Last in inward swift review
Strictly sifts the false and true?

Of these ample potencies
  Fitter cause, I ween,
Were Mind's self than marks impressed
  By the outer scene.
Yet the body through the sense
Stirs the soul's intelligence.

When light flashes on the eye,
  Or sound strikes the ear,
Mind aroused to due response
  Makes the message clear;
And the dumb external signs
With the hidden forms combines.

V.

'Now, although in the case of bodies endowed with sentiency the qualities of external objects affect the sense-organs, and the activity of mind is preceded by a bodily affection which calls forth the mind's action upon itself, and stimulates the forms till that moment lying inactive within, yet, I say, if in these bodies endowed with sentiency the mind is not inscribed by mere passive affection, but of its own efficacy discriminates the impressions furnished to the body, how much more do intelligences free from all bodily affections employ in their discrimination their own mental activities instead of conforming to external objects? So on these principles various modes of cognition belong to distinct and different substances. For to creatures void of motive power—shell-fish and other such creatures which cling to rocks and grow there—belongs

Sense alone, void of all other modes of gaining knowledge; to beasts endowed with movement, in whom some capacity of seeking and shunning seems to have arisen, Imagination also. Thought pertains only to the human race, as Intelligence to Divinity alone; hence it follows that that form of knowledge exceeds the rest which of its own nature cognizes not only its proper object, but the objects of the other forms of knowledge also. But what if Sense and Imagination were to gainsay Thought, and declare that universal which Thought deems itself to behold to be nothing? For the object of Sense and Imagination cannot be universal; so that either the judgment of Reason is true and there is no sense-object, or, since they know full well that many objects are presented to Sense and Imagination, the conception of Reason, which looks on that which is perceived by Sense and particular as if it were a something "universal," is empty of content. Suppose, further, that Reason maintains in reply that it does indeed contemplate the object of both Sense and Imagination under the form of universality, while Sense and Imagination cannot aspire to the knowledge of the universal, since their cognizance cannot go beyond bodily figures, and that in the cognition of reality we ought rather to trust the stronger and more perfect faculty of judgment. In a dispute of this sort, should not we, in whom is planted the faculty of reasoning as well as of imagining and perceiving, espouse the cause of Reason?

'In like manner is it that human reason thinks that Divine Intelligence cannot see the future except after the fashion in which its own knowledge is obtained. For thy contention is, if events do not appear to involve certain and necessary issues, they cannot be foreseen as certainly about to come to pass. There is, then, no foreknowledge of such events; or, if we can ever bring ourselves to believe that there is, there can be nothing which does not happen of necessity. If, however, we could have some part in the judgment of the Divine mind, even as we participate in Reason, we should think it perfectly just that human Reason should submit itself to the Divine mind, no less than we judged that Imagination and Sense ought to yield to Reason. Wherefore let us soar, if we can, to the heights of that Supreme Intelligence; for there Reason will see what in itself it cannot look upon; and that is in what way things whose occurrence is not certain may yet be seen in a sure and definite foreknowledge; and that this foreknowledge is not conjecture, but rather knowledge in its supreme simplicity, free of all limits and restrictions.'

SONG V.

The Upward Look.

In what divers shapes and fashions do the
    creatures great and small
Over wide earth's teeming surface skim,
    or scud, or walk, or crawl!
Some with elongated body sweep the
    ground, and, as they move,
Trail perforce with writhing belly in the
    dust a sinuous groove;

Some, on light wing upward soaring, swiftly
do the winds divide,
And through heaven's ample spaces in free
motion smoothly glide ;
These earth's solid surface pressing, with
firm paces onward rove,
Ranging through the verdant meadows,
crouching in the woodland grove.
Great and wondrous is their variance !
Yet in all the head low-bent
Dulls the soul and blunts the senses,
though their forms be different.
Man alone, erect, aspiring, lifts his fore-
head to the skies,
And in upright posture steadfast seems
earth's baseness to despise.
If with earth not all besotted, to this
parable give ear,
Thou whose gaze is fixed on heaven, who
thy face on high dost rear :
Lift thy soul, too, heavenward ; haply lest
it stain its heavenly worth,
And thine eyes alone look upward, while
thy mind cleaves to the earth !

VI.

'Since, then, as we lately proved, everything that is known is cognized not in accordance with its own nature, but in accordance with the nature of the faculty that comprehends it, let us now contemplate, as far as lawful, the character of the Divine essence, that we may be able to understand also the nature of its knowledge.

'God is eternal; in this judgment all rational beings agree. Let us, then, consider what eternity is. For this word carries with it a revelation alike of the Divine nature and of the Divine knowledge. Now, eternity is the possession of endless life whole and perfect at a single moment. What this is becomes more clear and manifest from a comparison with things temporal. For whatever lives in time is a present proceeding from the past to the future, and there is nothing set in time which can embrace the whole space of its life together. To-morrow's state it grasps not yet, while it has already lost yesterday's; nay, even in the life of to-day ye live no longer than one brief transitory moment. Whatever, therefore, is subject to the condition of time, although, as Aristotle deemed of the world, it never have either beginning or end, and its life be stretched to the whole extent of time's infinity, it yet is not such as rightly to be thought eternal. For it does not include and embrace the whole space of infinite life at once, but has no present hold on things to come, not yet accomplished. Accordingly, that which includes and possesses the whole fulness of unending life at once, from which nothing future is absent, from which nothing past has escaped, this is rightly called eternal; this must of necessity be ever present to itself in full self-possession, and hold the infinity of movable time in an abiding present. Wherefore they deem not rightly who imagine that on Plato's principles the created world is made co-eternal with the Creator, because they are told that he believed the world to have had no beginning in time,* and to be destined never to come to an end. For it is one thing for existence to be endlessly prolonged, which was what Plato ascribed to the world, another for the whole of an endless life to be embraced in the present, which is manifestly a property peculiar to the Divine mind. Nor need God appear earlier in mere duration of time to created things, but only prior in the unique simplicity of His nature. For the infinite progression of things in time copies this immediate existence in the present of the changeless life, and when it cannot succeed in equalling it, declines from movelessness into motion, and falls away from the simplicity of a perpetual present to the infinite duration of the future and the past; and since it cannot possess the whole fulness of its life together, for the very reason that in a manner it never ceases to be, it seems, up

* Plato expressly states the opposite in the 'Timæus' (28B), though possibly there the account of the beginning of the world in time is to be understood figuratively, not literally. See Jowett, vol. iii., pp. 448, 449 (3rd edit.).

to a certain point, to rival that which it cannot complete and express by attaching itself indifferently to any present moment of time, however swift and brief; and since this bears some resemblance to that ever-abiding present, it bestows on everything to which it is assigned the semblance of existence. But since it cannot abide, it hurries along the infinite path of time, and the result has been that it continues by ceaseless movement the life the completeness of which it could not embrace while it stood still. So, if we are minded to give things their right names, we shall follow Plato in saying that God indeed is eternal, but the world everlasting.

'Since, then, every mode of judgment comprehends its objects conformably to its own nature, and since God abides for ever in an eternal present, His knowledge, also transcending all movement of time, dwells in the simplicity of its own changeless present, and, embracing the whole infinite sweep of the past and of the future, contemplates all that falls within its simple cognition as if it were now taking place. And therefore, if thou wilt carefully consider that immediate presentment whereby it discriminates all things, thou wilt more rightly deem it not foreknowledge as of something future, but knowledge of a moment that never passes. For this cause the name chosen to describe it is not prevision, but providence, because, since utterly removed in nature from things mean and trivial, its outlook embraces all things as from some lofty height. Why, then, dost thou insist that the things which are surveyed by the Divine eye are involved in necessity, whereas clearly men impose no necessity on things which they see? Does the act of vision add any necessity to the things which thou seest before thy eyes?'

'Assuredly not.'

'And yet, if we may without unfitness compare God's present and man's, just as ye see certain things in this your temporary present, so does He see all things in His eternal present. Wherefore this Divine anticipation changes not the natures and properties of things, and it beholds things present before it, just as they will hereafter come to pass in time. Nor does it confound things in its judgment, but in the one mental view distinguishes alike what will come necessarily and what without necessity. For even as ye, when at one and the same time ye see a man walking on the earth and the sun rising in the sky, distinguish between the two, though one glance embraces both, and judge the former voluntary, the latter necessary action: so also the Divine vision in its universal range of view does in no wise confuse the characters of the things which are present to its regard, though future in respect of time. Whence it follows that when it perceives that something will come into existence, and yet is perfectly aware that this is unbound by any necessity, its apprehension is not opinion, but rather knowledge based on truth. And if to this thou sayest that what God sees to be about to come to pass cannot fail to come to pass, and that what cannot fail to come to pass happens of necessity, and wilt tie me down to this word necessity, I will acknowledge that thou affirmest a most solid truth, but one which scarcely anyone can approach to who has not made the

Divine his special study. For my answer would be that the same future event is necessary from the standpoint of Divine knowledge, but when considered in its own nature it seems absolutely free and unfettered. So, then, there are two necessities—one simple, as that men are necessarily mortal; the other conditioned, as that, if you know that someone is walking, he must necessarily be walking. For that which is known cannot indeed be otherwise than as it is known to be, and yet this fact by no means carries with it that other simple necessity. For the former necessity is not imposed by the thing's own proper nature, but by the addition of a condition. No necessity compels one who is voluntarily walking to go forward, although it is necessary for him to go forward at the moment of walking. In the same way, then, if Providence sees anything as present, that must necessarily be, though it is bound by no necessity of nature. Now, God views as present those coming events which happen of free will. These, accordingly, from the standpoint of the Divine vision are made necessary conditionally on the Divine cognizance; viewed, however, in themselves, they desist not from the absolute freedom naturally theirs. Accordingly, without doubt, all things will come to pass which God foreknows as about to happen, but of these certain proceed of free will; and though these happen, yet by the fact of their existence they do not lose their proper nature, in virtue of which before they happened it was really possible that they might not have come to pass.

'What difference, then, does the denial of necessity make, since, through their being conditioned by Divine knowledge, they come to pass as if they were in all respects under the compulsion of necessity? This difference, surely, which we saw in the case of the instances I formerly took, the sun's rising and the man's walking; which at the moment of their occurrence could not but be taking place, and yet one of them before it took place was necessarily obliged to be, while the other was not so at all. So likewise the things which to God are present without doubt exist, but some of them come from the necessity of things, others from the power of the agent. Quite rightly, then, have we said that these things are necessary if viewed from the standpoint of the Divine knowledge; but if they are considered in themselves, they are free from the bonds of necessity, even as everything which is accessible to sense, regarded from the standpoint of Thought, is universal, but viewed in its own nature particular. "But," thou wilt say, "if it is in my power to change my purpose, I shall make void providence, since I shall perchance change something which comes within its foreknowledge." My answer is: Thou canst indeed turn aside thy purpose; but since the truth of providence is ever at hand to see that thou canst, and whether thou dost, and whither thou turnest thyself, thou canst not avoid the Divine foreknowledge, even as thou canst not escape the sight of a present spectator, although of thy free will thou turn thyself to various actions. Wilt thou, then, say: "Shall the Divine knowledge be changed at my discretion, so that, when I will this or that, providence changes its knowledge correspondingly?"

'Surely not.'

'True, for the Divine vision anticipates all that is coming, and transforms and reduces it to the form of its own present knowledge, and varies not, as thou deemest, in its foreknowledge, alternating to this or that, but in a single flash it forestalls and includes thy mutations without altering. And this ever-present comprehension and survey of all things God has received, not from the issue of future events, but from the simplicity of His own nature. Hereby also is resolved the objection which a little while ago gave thee offence—that our doings in the future were spoken of as if supplying the cause of God's knowledge. For this faculty of knowledge, embracing all things in its immediate cognizance, has itself fixed the bounds of all things, yet itself owes nothing to what comes after.

'And all this being so, the freedom of man's will stands unshaken, and laws are not unrighteous, since their rewards and punishments are held forth to wills unbound by any necessity. God, who foreknoweth all things, still looks down from above, and the ever-present eternity of

His vision concurs with the future character of all our acts, and dispenseth to the good rewards, to the bad punishments. Our hopes and prayers also are not fixed on God in vain, and when they are rightly directed cannot fail of effect. Therefore, withstand vice, practise virtue, lift up your souls to right hopes, offer humble prayers to Heaven. Great is the necessity of righteousness laid upon you if ye will not hide it from yourselves, seeing that all your actions are done before the eyes of a Judge who seeth all things.'

EPILOGUE.

WITHIN a short time of writing 'The Consolation of Philosophy,' Boethius died by a cruel death. As to the manner of his death there is some uncertainty. According to one account, he was cut down by the swords of the soldiers before the very judgment-seat of Theodoric; according to another, a cord was first fastened round his forehead, and tightened till 'his eyes started'; he was then killed with a club.